HENRY! (16)

GERRARD! (22)

ROONEY! (28)

LAMPARD! (34)

(20)

PREM SUPERSTARS!

(40) **WICKED WINGERS!**

(56) **JOE COLE!**

(64) **JERMAINE JENAS!**

(68) **KIERAN RICHARDSON!**

(72) **BEST FOOTY MATES!**

(18) **MATCHMAN OF THE SEASON!**

WORLD CUP REVIEW! (44)

PACKED WITH FOOTY ACTION! →

D1145038

FORGETFUL
Duff

DID I SET THE VIDEO TO TAPE THE SIMPSONS? DOH!

OUCH!
WIGAN'S MIKE POLLITT NEEDS A PLASTER!

IT'S ONLY A LITTLE SCRATCH!

10 WAYS TO ENJOY THE

1

WEAR YOUR TEAM'S SHIRT!

2

DECORATE YOUR ROOM WITH COOL MATCH POSTERS!

3

BUST THE NET!

MAKE FRIENDS AND CHAT ON WWW.MATCHMAG.CO.UK

4

YOU GOTTA PICK SHEVA!

MANAGE A FANTASY LEAGUE TEAM WITH MATCH MEGASTARS!

5

TAKE IN AN EXCITING CHAMPIONS LEAGUE GAME!

4!

Goal! Goal! Goal! Goal! Yeah, whatever!

BLACKBURN STRIKER BENNI McCARTHY ONCE SCORED FOUR GOALS IN 13 MINUTES FOR SOUTH AFRICA DURING AN AFRICAN NATIONS CUP GAME AGAINST NAMIBIA!

GUESS THE PLAYER!

Can you name this Barcelona defender?

SEASON!

WANT TO MAKE THE MOST OF THE SEASON? JUST FOLLOW THE WICKED MATCH FOOTY GUIDE!

6 YOU ROCK, THIERRY!

JOIN YOUR JUNIOR SUPPORTERS CLUB!

7

LEARN A NEW FOOTY SONG!

SMALLEST HURDLE RACE.... EVER!

I WIN! YIPPEE!

CHECK OUT THIS CRAZY MINI-HURDLE RACE! ARE THEY GOING FOR A WORLD RECORD?

8

GUESS WHO WILL WIN THE TROPHIES!

9

JOIN YOUR LOCAL TEAM!

CELEBRATE LIKE...

RONALDINHO

1

SCORE A WONDER GOAL!

2

HIGH-FIVE THE TEAM!

SHAKE IT BABY, SHAKE IT!

10

WATCH YOUR TEAM PRACTISE AT THEIR TRAINING GROUND!

3

SHOW YOUR TEETH AND WAVE YOUR FINGERS!

BLOW-UP TROPHY!
Check out this crazy inflatable cup!

GET IN THERE, BARTON!

CELEBRITY FOOTY FANS!
England cricketer Andrew Flintoff supports Man. City!

DAVID BECK

HIS WICKED

1992
NEW CLASS!
Becks was in the same youth team as Gary and Phil Neville, Paul Scholes, Nicky Butt and Robbie Savage at Man. United!

1997
MAN. UNITED STAR!
By 1997, Becks was one of the best players in the Prem, and bagged loads of goals for United!

1998
WORLD CUP SHAME!
Becks suffered his darkest moment when he was sent off against Argentina as England crashed out of the World Cup!

1992   1993   1994   1995   1996   1997   1998   1999   2000   2001

I'M SO HAPPY I'M GONNA SING, DAVID!

PLEASE DON'T, VICKY!

1999
TREBLE LEGEND!
David played a vital role as United won the Premiership, FA Cup and the Champions League treble! Amazing!

1995
BECKS DEBUT!
David made his first Prem appearance for Man. United against Leeds on April 2, 1995!

1998
POSH AND BECKS!
Away from footy, Becks met pop star Posh Spice – who soon became Victoria Beckham!

HAIR WE GO!
Beckham's best haircuts!

MESSY!

FLOPPY!

HIGHLIGHTS!

SHAVED!

MOHAWK!

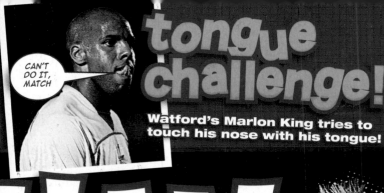

tongue challenge!

Watford's Marlon King tries to touch his nose with his tongue!

"CAN'T DO IT, MATCH"

HAM CAREER!

YEP, I'VE WON LOADS OF MEDALS!

He's one of England's most famous players ever, so MATCH looks back at Beckham's awesome career!

BECKS' BOOTS!

Becks is a cool dude and he's had some wicked boots over the years!

2001 ENGLAND HERO!

Becks scored a vital free-kick against Greece to send England to the 2002 World Cup finals!

2002 ARGIE BARGIE!

Beckham got his revenge over Argentina by scoring the vital penalty in a 1-0 win at the 2002 World Cup! Get in!

ENGLAND

2002 2003 2004 2005 2006

2003 REAL DEAL!

In 2003, Becks moved to Spanish club Real Madrid for a whopping £25 million! United fans were gutted!

NICE SUIT, BECKS!

BECKHAM 23

GIRLY!

2006 WORLD CUP TEARS!

Becks helped England to the World Cup quarter-finals, but got injured as England lost. Then he quit as captain!

BRAIDED!

SPIKEY!

PLANET FOOTY!

WHO'S TALLER?

ASHLEY COLE OR **EDGAR DAVIDS?**

ANSWER: Ashley Cole 5ft 8ins, Edgar Davids 5ft 7ins.

DID YOU KNOW...?

ARSENAL'S ALL-TIME RECORD GOALSCORER THIERRY HENRY FAILED TO SCORE IN HIS FIRST TEN GAMES FOR THE CLUB!

HENRY 14

Arsenal

PREMIERSHIP A-Z!

The Premiership is the best league in the world – and here's why!

F

...is for Fans!
You guys rock! Prem supporters go nuts for their fave team!

SING UP FOR THE LADS!

G

...is for Goals, goals, goals!
Thierry Henry scores goals for fun! How many will he bag in 2006-07?

A

...is for Attendances!
The average Prem attendance is 33,875! Man. United get crowds of more than 75,000!

C

...is for Champions!
Chelsea, Arsenal, Man. United and Blackburn have all won the Prem since it began in 1992!

H

MULLINS 17

...is for Huge scraps!
The action can get a bit tasty! Watch out for mega rumbles!

D

THE REDS RULE!

...is for Derbies!
The Prem's packed with red-hot rivalries and wicked derbies! Liverpool v Everton, Arsenal v Spurs and United v City are mega!

I

...is for Injury-time!
If the fourth official flashes up loads of injury-time, your team will want to score again!

B

...is for Bling boots!
Forget boring, plain black boots – the Premiership is full of blinged up colours and styles!

E

...is for Emirates Stadium!
Arsenal's flash new home is one of the best in the world!

J

...is for Jumping!
Somersault celebrations from fellas like Lomana Lua Lua are awesome!

FOOTY TERMS!

"RUNNING DOWN THE CLOCK!"
When a game is about to finish and a team wants to protect their lead, they'll 'run down the clock' by keeping the ball in the corners and wasting time!

MONEY MAKERS!

Who has been bought for small change and sold for big cash?

MICHAEL CARRICK
Bought for £2.75 million by Spurs
Sold for £18.6 million to Man. United
Profit: £15.85 million!

DEAN ASHTON
Bought for £3 million by Norwich
Sold for £7.25 million to West Ham
Profit: £4.25 million!

ANDY JOHNSON
Bought for £750,000 by Palace
Sold for £8.6 million to Everton
Profit: £7.85 million!

K

...is for 'Keepers!
Liverpool's Jose Reina kept 20 clean sheets last year!

P

...is for Penalties!
In 2005-06, 78 pens were given – and 57 were scored!

T

...is for Transfers!
The world's top stars want to play in the Prem! It's great when clubs splash the cash!

U

...is for Unsung heroes!
They're not superstars, but do an awesome job!

L

...is for Ledley King!
King scored the fastest Prem goal – after 10 seconds in 2000!

Q

...is for Quality free-kicks!
Look out for some sweet 30-yard free-kicks!

V

...is for Volleys!
Watch out for some wicked volleys hitting the back of the net!

M

I'M WELL MINTED!

...is for Mega money!
The newspapers reckon Chelsea's Michael Ballack gets £120,000 a week!

R

...is for Referee!
Everybody loves to hate the men in black!

W

...is for Winning!
Who'll lift the Prem trophy in May?

X

...is for X-Rated!
Don't get scared of tough tackles and battles!

N

...is for New boys!
Reading, Sheffield United and Watford love playing against the big boys!

S

Y

...is for Yellow cards!
Everton's Phil Neville got 12 yellow cards last season! Terrible!

O

...is for Own goals!
It's cruel, but you've gotta laugh when a defender slices the ball into his own net!

...is for Superstitions!
Some players have got crazy superstitions, like kissing trophies when they win it!

Z

GIMME SOME MEDALS!

...is for Zokora!
Tottenham's powerful midfielder wants to win trophies!

PLANET FOOTY!

£100m!

That's how much it will cost to buy Ronaldinho from Barcelona! It's written into his contract!

MATCHY'S DICTIONARY!

Fergie. adj. Angry. From United boss Alex Ferguson. E.g. "John forgot to do his homework and the teacher was well Fergie!"

THE ULTIMATE SUPERKID!

Imagine if you could take all the best bits from the planet's top youngsters to make one wicked player! MATCH did, and here's what he looks like...

YOU CAN'T STOP ME!

HEAD!

PER MERTESACKER! Germany's World Cup star is a big old unit and wins everything in the air! He'd be the perfect head!

BRAIN!

LIONEL MESSI! Cheeky Barcelona trickster Messi has the vision to open up any defence, so he's the perfect choice to be our player's brain!

BODY!

JOHN OBI MIKEL! Mikel's only been at Chelsea a few months, but he's got bags of talent and his super strength makes him our body!

ARMS!

OSCAR USTARI! Young Argentina 'keeper Ustari is an awesome shot stopper with great handling, so who better to be the arms?

LEGS!

THEO WALCOTT! Theo is as fast as Thierry Henry, and all the best players need pace! Walcott's speedy legs get the nod!

RIGHT FOOT!

CESC FABREGAS! Fabregas can play a perfect pass or let rip with a rocket shot! He's in as our wonderkid's right boot!

LEFT FOOT!

LUKAS PODOLSKI! The Germany ace was voted the best young player at the World Cup! His left foot rocks!

YOUNG GUNS!

Take a look at MATCH's World Superkids team! Do you agree with our choices? Write down which players you'd pick in your ultimate team of youngsters!

THE LINE-UP!

PICK YOUR TEAM OF WORLD WONDERKIDS!

OSCAR USTARI

GOALKEEPER
Age: 20
Club: Independiente
Country: Argentina
I WOULD PICK:

. . . .

SERGIO RAMOS

RIGHT-BACK
Age: 20
Club: Real Madrid
Country: Spain
I WOULD PICK:

. . . .

PER MERTESACKER

CENTRE-BACK
Age: 22
Club: W. Bremen
Country: Germany
I WOULD PICK:

. . . .

ASSIMIOU TOURE

CENTRE-BACK
Age: 19
Club: B. Leverkusen
Country: Togo
I WOULD PICK:

. . . .

MARCELL JANSEN

LEFT-BACK
Age: 20
Club: B. M'gladbach
Country: Germany
I WOULD PICK:

. . . .

AARON LENNON

RIGHT-WING
Age: 19
Club: Tottenham
Country: England
I WOULD PICK:

. . . .

CESC FABREGAS

MIDFIELDER
Age: 19
Club: Arsenal
Country: Spain
I WOULD PICK:

. . . .

JOHN OBI MIKEL

MIDFIELDER
Age: 18
Club: Chelsea
Country: Nigeria
I WOULD PICK:

. . . .

LIONEL MESSI

LEFT-WING
Age: 19
Club: Barcelona
Country: Argentina
I WOULD PICK:

. . . .

THEO WALCOTT

STRIKER
Age: 17
Club: Arsenal
Country: England
I WOULD PICK:

. . . .

LUKAS PODOLSKI

STRIKER
Age: 21
Club: Bayern Munich
Country: Germany
I WOULD PICK:

. . . .

AVERAGE AGE: 19!

STEVIE G DOES YOGA!

OW! THIS WELL HURTS!

IF HE WAS A RAPPER RIO FERDINAND WOULD BE...

R Unit

CHECK OUT MY DOPE RHYMES!

PREMIERSHIP

THIS IS AS FAST AS I CAN GO!

SOL CAMPBELL!
CLUB: PORTSMOUTH
SPORT: WALKING
MEDAL CHANCE: BRONZE

HEY REF, HE PUSHED ME!

CRISTIANO RONALDO!
CLUB: MAN. UNITED
SPORT: DIVING
MEDAL CHANCE: GOLD

Which event would these Prem stars compete in if they were at the Olympics?

I FEEL SICK!

LOMANA LUA LUA!
CLUB: PORTSMOUTH
SPORT: GYMNASTICS
MEDAL CHANCE: GOLD

OLYMPICS!

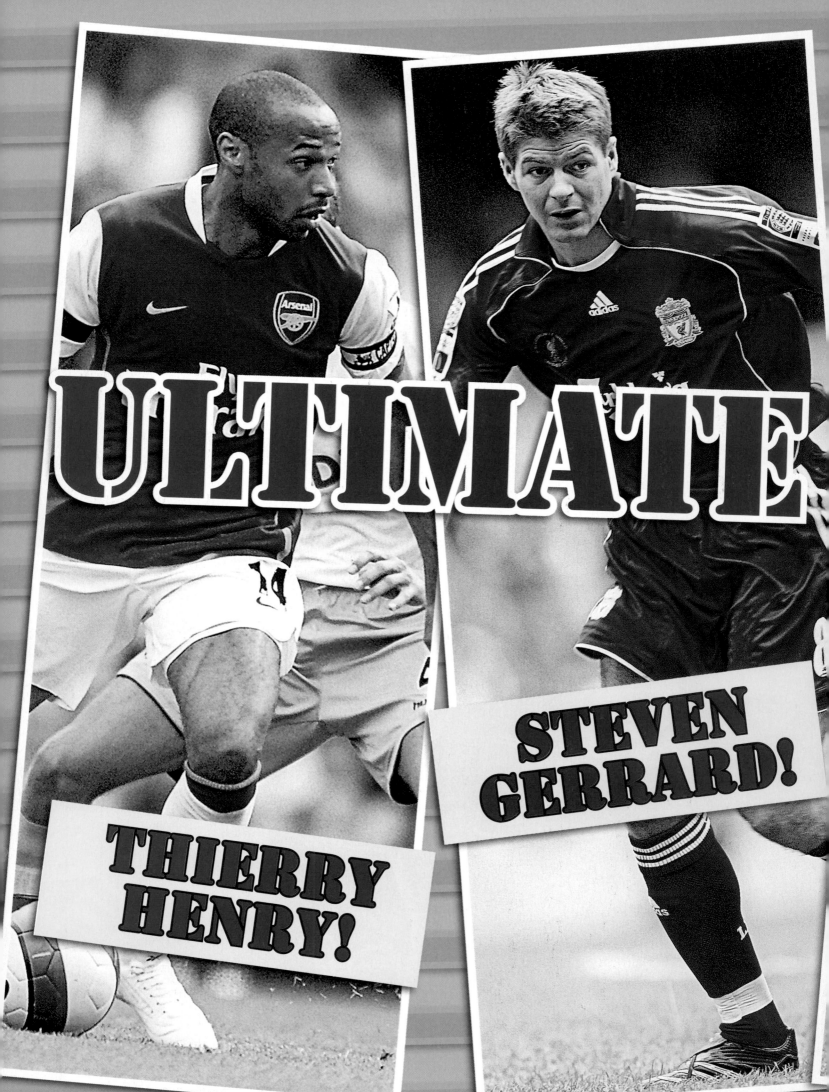

ULTIMATE

THIERRY HENRY!

STEVEN GERRARD!

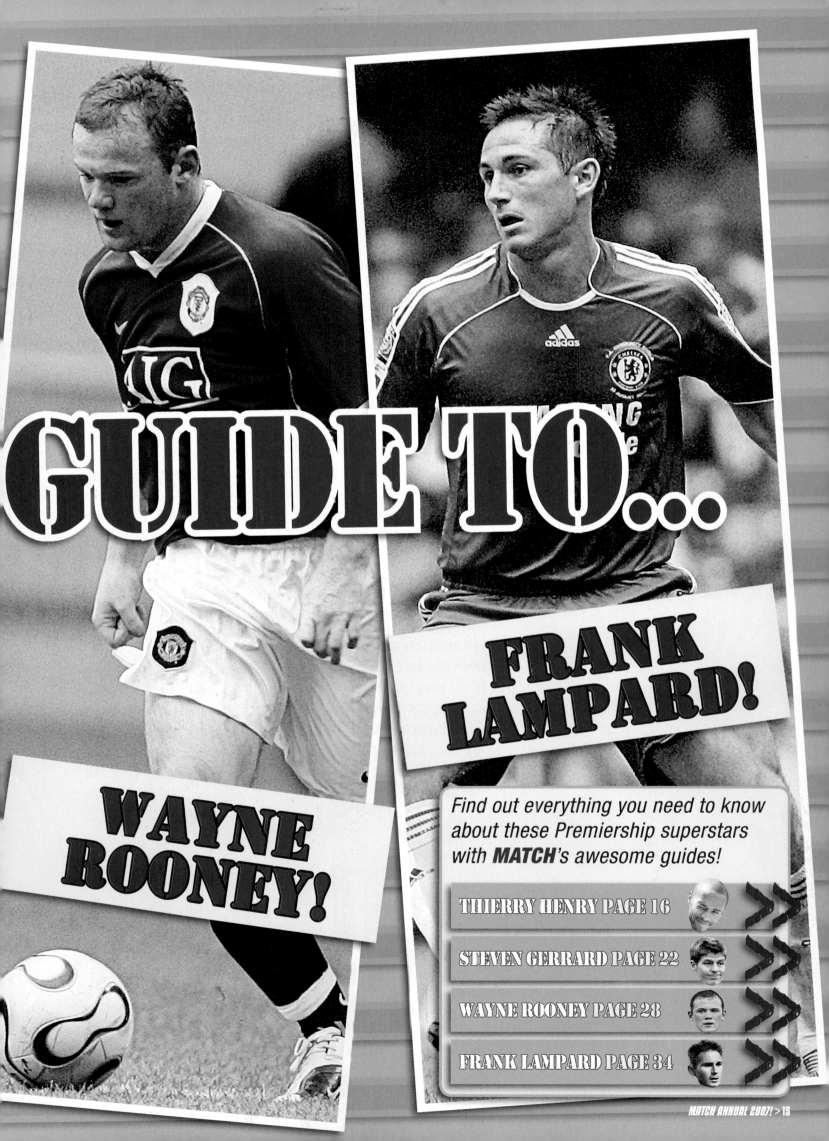

GUIDE TO...

FRANK LAMPARD!

WAYNE ROONEY!

Find out everything you need to know about these Premiership superstars with **MATCH**'s awesome guides!

Thierry Daniel Henry was born on August 17, 1977, in Paris! Even by the age of six he was fab – he was picked for France's famous Clairefontaine academy!

Henry made his debut as a winger for Monaco in 1994 – when he was 17! His boss back then was Arsene Wenger!

MONACO MAGIC!

ULTIMATE GUIDE TO...

THIERRY

Henry got a £10.7 million move to Juventus in 1999 – but it all went wrong! Seven months, 12 games and just three goals later, he packed his bags to rejoin Wenger at Arsenal!

Henry's magic feet do the talking on the pitch, but off it he's pretty special too! He can speak French, English and Italian!

ARSENAL'S MAN!

HENRY
14

He made his France debut in 1997 against South Africa! Since then, he's played in an amazing three World Cups, plus Euro 2000 and Euro 2004!

FRENCH FANCY!

HENRY!

In October 2005, Henry became Arsenal's all-time top scorer! His two strikes against Sparta Prague meant he overtook Ian Wright's record of 185 goals!

GOAL LEGEND!

Despite talk linking him with a big move to Spanish champs Barcelona, Arsenal fans were well chuffed at the end of last season when Henry signed a new deal to stay with The Gunners!

ULTIMATE GUIDE TO...
THIERRY HENRY!

HIGHBURY LEGEND!

Henry scored the last goals at Highbury before The Gunners moved to the Emirates Stadium – a hat-trick against Wigan!

Last season, his awesome displays for Arsenal saw him scoop MATCHMAN Of The Month awards in November and March! Thierry said he'd put them with all the other awards he'd won!

He became a big TV star when he starred in the famous 'Va Va Voom' Renault Clio adverts! He made the word so popular, it's now in the English dictionary!

Thierry announced himself to the world by firing France to World Cup glory in 1998! He was the team's top scorer with three goals from six games!

WORLD CUP WINNER!

Arsenal are said to have rejected two bids of £50 million, thought to be from Spanish clubs, for Thierry before he signed a new deal! Henry would have become the world's most expensive star!

He's won the Football Writers' Footballer Of The Year award three times, the PFA Players' Player Of The Year twice, and the French Player Of The Year on a record four occasions!

RECORD BREAKER!

Henry's scored over 20 Prem goals every season from 2002 to 2006, and has twice won the Euro Golden Boot!

PLANET FOOTY!

HIP-HOP SAM!

"Yo, yo, yo! Waddup?"

Bolton boss Sam Allardyce acts like his fave rap stars!

FOOTY TERMS!

"HOLD THE LINE!"

When a team is defending, the back four will try to 'hold the line'. This means they will stay in a perfect line to see if they can catch a striker offside! Clever!

BEST OF...
CAUGHT ON CAMERA!

MAKE ME FLY!

Ronaldo's mum makes him come in for his tea!

Girly headband!

HEY, I LOVE YOU! KISS, KISS!

NO! WANNA PLAY FOOTY, MUM!

Ronaldinho really does love football!

Rocket boots?

Cry baby!

Chelsea's SWP will do anything to be taller!

Big bully!

WILL DO.

GIMME THE BALL!

Works in Maccy D's?

I THINK YOU'RE CRAZY...

Nobody messes with an angry Edgar Davids!

YUM!

Quick snack?

Premiership refs can't stop singing!

Newcastle need to feed their players more!

MATCH!

RONALDINHO
BRAZIL

Unlike fellow Liverpool heroes Robbie Fowler and Jamie Carragher, who supported Everton when they were young, Stevie was always a fan of The Reds!

Gerrard always loved playing footy as a youngster! When he was at secondary school in Liverpool, he used to go on scouting missions to spy on other schools' teams to see how good they were!

ULTIMATE GUIDE TO...

STEVEN

Stevie G was named in England's squad for the Euro 2000 finals! He played in the brilliant 1-0 win over Germany – the first time we had beaten them in a competitive game since 1966!

At Liverpool, Gerrard has won the FA Cup twice in 2006 and 2001, the League Cup in 2003 and 2001, the UEFA Cup in 2001 and the Champions League in 2005! Loads of medals!

ENGLAND GLORY!

LEAGUE DEBUT!

The midfielder made his Liverpool debut as a substitute against Blackburn on November 30, 1998, before making his full debut against Celta Vigo in the UEFA Cup two weeks later!

Gerrard came through the England youth set-up and played four under-21 games! He made his full England debut in an ace 2-0 win against Ukraine in 2000 – the day after his 20th birthday!

GERRARD!

TROPHY-TASTIC!

The Reds' captain was all set to join Chelsea in the summer of 2005, but he turned them down at the last minute! He loves Liverpool that much!

The only club trophy Stevie hasn't won is the Premiership! Watch out Chelsea – he's desperate to change that!

ULTIMATE GUIDE TO...
STEVEN GERRARD!

ENGLAND 5-1 GERMANY!

In 2001, Stevie was PFA Young Player Of The Year as Liverpool won the League Cup, the FA Cup and the UEFA Cup! He even scored in the 4-3 UEFA Cup final win over Alaves!

Gerrard bagged his first England goal in the 5-1 whupping of Germany in September 2001! It was a wicked shot from 25 yards which flew into the net and gave The Three Lions a 2-1 lead!

Last season, Gerrard was Liverpool's top scorer with 23 goals from 53 matches – nearly a goal every other game! Not bad for a midfielder!

FA CUP FINAL SCREAMER!

When he netted twice in the 2006 FA Cup final win over West Ham, it meant Stevie had scored in all four major cup finals – the League Cup, FA Cup, UEFA Cup and Champions League!

When Stevie G won the Champions League, he became the second youngest captain ever to lift the trophy! Only Didier Deschamps has been a younger skipper!

Stevie says his best – and most important – goal was against Olympiakos in the Champions League. The Reds needed to win by two goals, and Gerrard smashed home a 25-yarder to seal a 3-1 win!

CHAMPO LEAGUE HERO!

In 2006, Stevie was named **PFA Player Of The Year!** He beat Wayne Rooney, Frank Lampard and Thierry Henry to the award, and became the first Liverpool player to win it since John Barnes in 1988!

WORLD CUP DEBUT!

Stevie made his first World Cup finals appearance in the 1-0 win over Paraguay last summer. He was England's top scorer too, with goals against Trinidad & Tobago and Sweden!

CHEEKY NUTMEG!

In one of his first training sessions with the Liverpool first team, Stevie nutmegged then captain and England star Paul Ince. 'The Guvnor' wasn't happy about it, though!

 **CHAMPS & CHUMPS!**

Which of these teams haven't won the Prem? Tick the champs and cross the chumps!

Tottenham	Man. United	Arsenal	Liverpool	Chelsea

YES! ☐ NO! ☐	YES! ☐ NO! ☐	YES! ☐ NO! ☐	YES! ☐ NO! ☐	YES! ☐ NO! ☐

THE NEXT BIG THING!

MAN. CITY wonderkid DANIEL STURRIDGE is one of England's biggest footy talents! MATCH meets the 17-year-old who is ready to set the Premiership alight!

WATCH OUT FOR ME, MATCH FANS!

MEGA FACT!
He won the 'Most Valuable Player' prize as City's under-16s were crowned world club champions in 2004!

MEGA FACT!
Daniel's first club was Cadbury Athletic! They played outside the gates of a huge chocolate factory in Birmingham!

DANIEL STURRIDGE!

CLUB: Man. City
AGE: 17
POSITION: Striker
ENGLAND RECORD:
Under-16: Games: 4, Goals: 5
Under-17: Games: 9, Goals: 5
TOP SKILL: Scoring wicked long-range screamers!
KICKING FOOT: Left!

The powerful striker signed a massive sponsorship deal with sportswear giant Adidas when he was just 13!

Sturridge joined City from Coventry after ripping the team apart in a game when he was just 13 years old!

MEGA FACT!
Sturridge had a wicked partnership with Theo Walcott for the England Under-16 and Under-17 teams!

MEGA FACT!
The striker scored two goals, including a 25-yard beauty, in the 2006 FA Youth Cup final against Liverpool!

DANIEL ON...

...HIS STRENGTHS!
"My finishing is definitely a strength, and my shooting from outside the box is very good too. I've always had those skills in my game!"

...THE FIRST TEAM!
"The future looks bright for the club with so many players stepping up from the youth team. My aim is to break through this season!"

...CAREER HIGH!
"Winning the Nike World Tournament with Man. City's Under-16s was brilliant! Teams like Barcelona and Corinthians were playing there too, but we won!"

...THE BRAZILIANS!
"I'm a huge fan of Brazilian football – I've tried to model my game on the way they play. I went to Switzerland last summer to watch some of their training sessions!"

...HIS DREAM!
"To play with Wayne Rooney and Theo Walcott at full international level. I'll have to see if it happens!"

WORLD SUPERSTARS!

ANDRIY SHEVCHENKO
UKRAINE

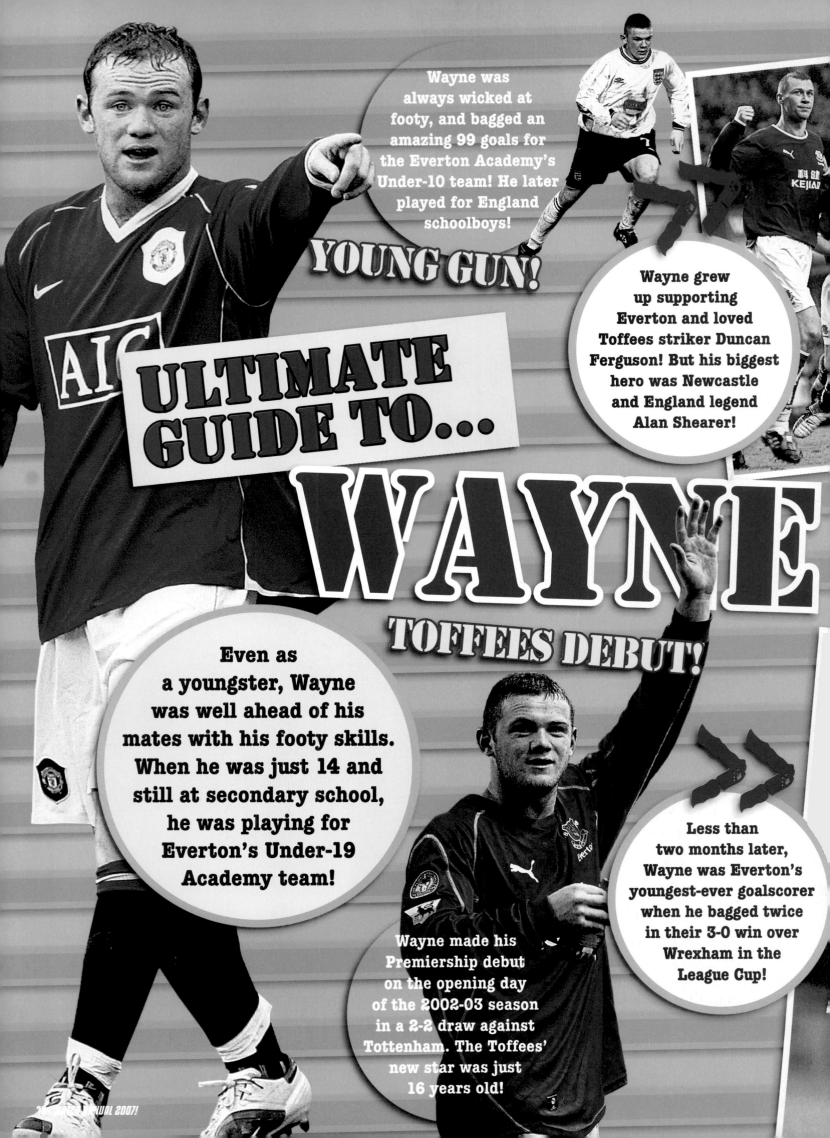

Wayne was always wicked at footy, and bagged an amazing 99 goals for the Everton Academy's Under-10 team! He later played for England schoolboys!

YOUNG GUN!

Wayne grew up supporting Everton and loved Toffees striker Duncan Ferguson! But his biggest hero was Newcastle and England legend Alan Shearer!

ULTIMATE GUIDE TO...

WAYNE

TOFFEES DEBUT!

Even as a youngster, Wayne was well ahead of his mates with his footy skills. When he was just 14 and still at secondary school, he was playing for Everton's Under-19 Academy team!

Wayne made his Premiership debut on the opening day of the 2002-03 season in a 2-2 draw against Tottenham. The Toffees' new star was just 16 years old!

Less than two months later, Wayne was Everton's youngest-ever goalscorer when he bagged twice in their 3-0 win over Wrexham in the League Cup!

Wayne became England's youngest-ever player when he made his debut against Australia in 2003, aged just 17 years and 111 days! But Arsenal's Theo Walcott broke the record in 2006!

Rooney bagged his first England goal in a 2-1 win against Macedonia in September 2003 to become England's youngest-ever scorer! The striker was just 17 years and 317 days old!

ROONEY!

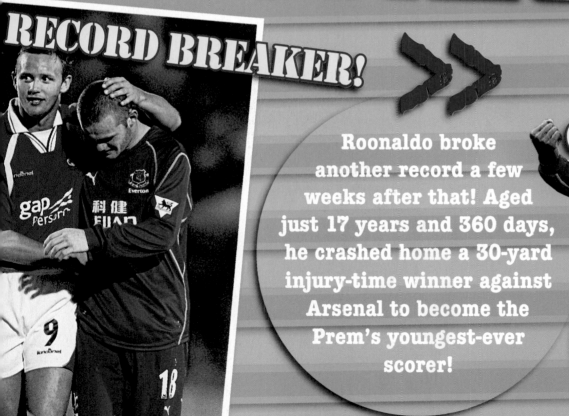

RECORD BREAKER!

Roonaldo broke another record a few weeks after that! Aged just 17 years and 360 days, he crashed home a 30-yard injury-time winner against Arsenal to become the Prem's youngest-ever scorer!

GUNNERS FIRED DOWN!

Wayne loves chilling out to music, and two of his fave stars are Eminem and Kanye West! He also loves boxing, with fighting legend Mike Tyson a hero!

ULTIMATE GUIDE TO...
WAYNE ROONEY!

EURO STAR!

Roonaldo hit four goals in his first three games at Euro 2004! He was only 18, but he became the youngest-ever scorer at the finals and shot himself to fame on the world stage!

£30 MILLION TRANSFER!

After his wicked Euro 2004, Wayne swapped Everton for Man. United in a £30 million deal to become the world's most expensive teenager!

Wayne will never forget his Red Devils debut! It was against Fenerbahce in the Champions League, and United's new hitman smashed a hat-trick in a 6-2 whupping!

DREAM DEBUT!

In 2005, after an ace first season at Man. United and top displays for England, Wayne won the first-ever FIFPro World Young Player Of The Year award!

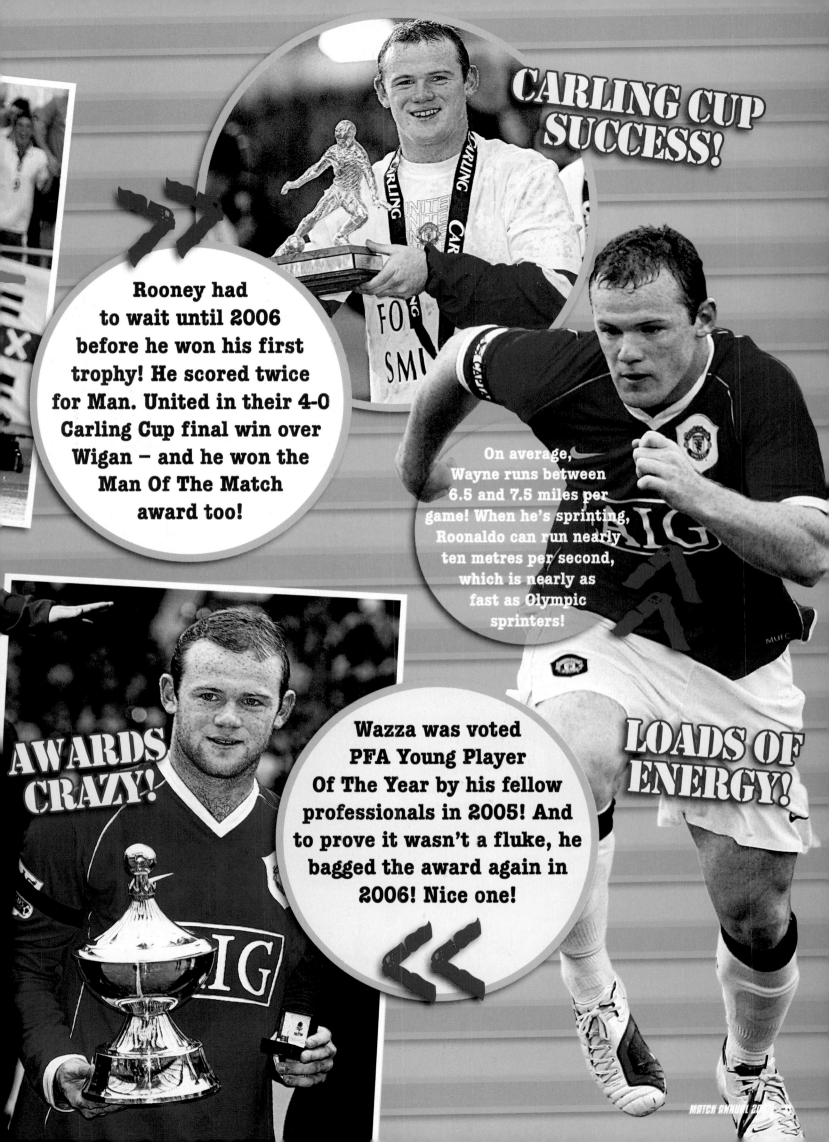

CARLING CUP SUCCESS!

Rooney had to wait until 2006 before he won his first trophy! He scored twice for Man. United in their 4-0 Carling Cup final win over Wigan – and he won the Man Of The Match award too!

On average, Wayne runs between 6.5 and 7.5 miles per game! When he's sprinting, Roonaldo can run nearly ten metres per second, which is nearly as fast as Olympic sprinters!

LOADS OF ENERGY!

AWARDS CRAZY!

Wazza was voted PFA Young Player Of The Year by his fellow professionals in 2005! And to prove it wasn't a fluke, he bagged the award again in 2006! Nice one!

FEELING THE HEAT!
Didier Drogba
Chelsea

I'M BOILING, MATCH!

MY OTHER SPORT!
Scott Parker
Newcastle
Footy Volleyball

BEST OF...
CAUGHT ON CAMERA!

The stars can't escape from MATCH's secret cameras!

Where are the fans?

HA! YOU'LL NEVER FIND ME!

Fulham play a bit of hide and seek!

Smelt it, dealt it?

ARGH, THAT STINKS!

Gaz Southgate smells big trouble at Boro!

ME CHEWING GUM HAS EXPLODED! ARGH!

Hubba Bubba lover!

Bolton's Ricardo Vaz Te is in a sticky situation!

I CAN'T HEAR YOU!

False teeth?

Zamora's turning into an old man!

CAN I GO HOME NOW?

Not interested!

Bit interested!

Very interested!

WORLD SUPERSTARS!

MATCH!

FRANK RIBERY
FRANCE

Franky Lamps joined Chelsea from West Ham back in 2001 for a massive £11 million! The ace midfielder was one of Blues boss Claudio Ranieri's first signings, and was given the No.8 shirt!

ENGLAND UNDER-21 DEBUT!

Lamps made his England Under-21 debut in 1997! He played 19 games in total and was made captain as well!

ULTIMATE GUIDE TO...

FRANK

The goalscoring king scored his 100th career goal in 2003! He cracked in a late equaliser for Chelsea against Arsenal in the FA Cup sixth round, but The Blues lost the replay 3-1!

HAMMER TIME!

He made his full England debut in 1999 against Belgium, and scored his first goal against Croatia in 2003. He was voted 2004 England Player Of The Year by the fans!

When he was a teenager, Lampard went to a posh private school in Essex! He's a clever lad and worked hard, so mum and dad sent him to the £10,000-a-year Brentwood School!

His dad was a footy star too! Frank Senior played for West Ham in the 1970s, and Frank's uncle is Pompey boss Harry Redknapp!

FOOTY FAMILY!

597-05

LAMPARD!

MATCHMAN OF THE MONTH!

CHEL

His first game for West Ham was in January 1996! He played more than 200 games for The Hammers with stars like Joe Cole, Rio Ferdinand and Michael Carrick!

Frank won a wicked MATCH award in January 2006! The Chelsea hero was crowned MATCHMAN Of The Month, and he was well chuffed to land the prize and speak to his fave footy mag!

FRANK LAMPARD!

Lamps joined West Ham when he was a boy and worked his way through the youth teams! He was loaned out to Swansea in 1995 and played 11 games for the Welsh club, scoring one goal!

WORLD CUP DEBUT!

EURO 2004 HERO!

Lampard made his World Cup debut in 2006! He played in all of England's five games, but didn't score!

The Chelsea fave is a big Adidas superstar! He wears awesome Adidas footy boots and looks well cool in the new 2006-07 Adidas Chelsea kit!

Lamps set a Premiership record last season! After playing 164 games in a row for Chelsea, he was given a special award! Time for a rest, Franky!

WORLD CLASS!

He was crowned runner-up in the 2005 FIFA World Player Of The Year awards! Even though he scored loads of amazing goals for club and country, Lamps was just beaten to top spot by Ronaldinho!

Frank became a big England star at Euro 2004 in Portugal! He scored three goals in just four games, and was easily one of the best players at the tournament!

BABY LAMPS!

Lamps has a baby girl called Luna Coco Patricia! His fianceé is a tasty Spanish lady called Elen Rives!

5 TOP STRIKERS!

These goal machines don't need any tips to hit the back of the net!

THIERRY HENRY! ARSENAL

ANDRIY SHEVCHENKO! CHELSEA

MIROSLAV KLOSE! WERDER BREMEN

RUUD VAN NISTELROOY! REAL MADRID

LUCA TONI! FIORENTINA

HOW TO...
BEAT THE 'KEEPER!

We all love scoring goals! MATCH tells you everything you need to know about banging 'em in when you're one-on-one with the 'keeper!

1 GO ROUND HIM!

Get past the 'keeper and it's an open goal! Drop your shoulder one way, as if you were about to go that side, but then push the ball the other way instead! 1-0!

2 FAKE!

If you make the 'keeper commit himself, then you can pick your spot! Bring your leg back as if you're shooting, then at the last second, push the ball away from the 'keeper. He should be on the floor – an easy goal!

3 BOTTOM CORNER!

To hit the bottom corner, you can either go for power and smash it, or go for accuracy and place it! Use the inside of your foot to curl it past the 'keeper, or lean over it and strike through for power!

4 TOP CORNER!

It's tough to do, but you'll probably score if you get it right! You can use the top of your boot or the inside of your boot, depending on which foot you use. But hit the right spot and it's in!

5 THROUGH THE LEGS!

This is all about timing! Wait for the goalkeeper to move towards you, then slip the ball through his legs. And if you don't score, you might knock the rebound in!

6 THE CHIP!

The most difficult of all – you'll need confidence to go for this! As the 'keeper runs at you, bring your leg back to shoot, then dig your foot under the ball and chip it over him. Don't lean too far back, because it will fly over!

WORLD SUPERSTARS!

WAYNE ROONEY
ENGLAND

FREDDIE LJUNGBERG
Age: 29
Club: Arsenal
Country: Sweden
Top skill: Runs into the box!

SWP says: "He's great at timing his runs to get in behind the back four! He's a good dribbler, likes to play one-twos and is a very confident finisher!"

ARJEN ROBBEN
Age: 22
Club: Chelsea
Country: Holland
Top skill: Dribbling!

SWP says: "The way he's so cool in front of goal is unbelievable for a winger! When he's dribbling, the ball just seems to stick to his foot. It's so hard to get the ball off him!"

SHAUN WRIGHT-PHILLIPS' GUIDE TO...
WICKED WI

DAVID BECKHAM
Age: 31
Club: Real Madrid
Country: England
Top skill: Crossing!

SWP says: "He's not an out-and-out winger, but Becks is a great player! He tries to set other people up to score and he's happy if he plays well and creates chances!"

HARRY KEWELL
Age: 28
Club: Liverpool
Country: Australia
Top skill: Volleys!

SWP says: "His left foot is like a wand! He's a great player and he gives his team options. He creates, he shoots and he swaps wings. He's very hard to stop!"

ROBINHO
Age: 22
Club: Real Madrid
Country: Brazil
Top skill: Tricks!

SWP says: "He's a very, very good player! I've been watching him on TV! He's a bit like Cristiano Ronaldo in that he's got tricks, but he's composed too!"

CRISTIANO RONALDO
Age: 21
Club: Man. United
Country: Portugal
Top skill: Stepovers!

SWP says: "He's very skilful and always seems to beat his man! He's quick, but his tricks can send defenders the wrong way and that can give him a head start, too!"

NGERS!

CHELSEA & ENGLAND winger SWP tells MATCH all about his fave wing wizards!

PAVEL NEDVED
Age: 34
Club: Juventus
Country: Czech Republic
Top skill: Two good feet!

SWP says: "He's a direct winger! He's not really a player who likes to do a lot of tricks. He likes to play one-twos and create chances for his team-mates!"

JOE COLE
Age: 24
Club: Chelsea
Country: England
Top skill: Quick feet!

SWP says: "If he gets the defender on the back foot, he'll beat them every time! He can go left or right to get past the defender and is up with the best in the world!"

MATCHMAN'S... PREMIERSHIP QUIZ!

MY SCORE /60

NEXT QUIZ PAGE 54

ANSWERS PAGE 92-93

THE KNOWLEDGE!

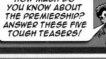

HOW MUCH DO YOU KNOW ABOUT THE PREMIERSHIP? ANSWER THESE FIVE TOUGH TEASERS!

1 Which striker, who hung up his boots last season, is the Premiership's all-time leading scorer?

ANSWER

2 Four Premiership clubs have 'United' in their name, but how many have 'Athletic'?

ANSWER

3 Arsenal, Chelsea, Everton, Liverpool, Man. United & Tottenham have all been in the Premiership since 1992, but which other team has as well?

ANSWER

4 Where must a team finish in the table to be able to qualify for the Champions League?

ANSWER

Position	Team	Played	GD	Points
1	Chelsea	38	50	91
2	Man Utd	38	38	83
3	Liverpool	38	32	82
4	Arsenal	38	37	67
5	Tottenham	38	15	65
6	Blackburn	38	9	63
7	Newcastle	38	5	58

5 Only four teams have ever won the Premiership – Man. United, Arsenal, Chelsea and which other club, way back in 1995?

ANSWER

2 POINTS FOR EACH CORRECT ANSWER

MY SCORE /10

PERCY'S PLAYERS!

HELP ME WORK OUT WHO THIS SILLY SAUSAGE IS! THE THINGY COVERING HIS FACE IS A BIG CLUE TO HIS NAME!

ANSWER

10 POINTS FOR CORRECT ANSWER

MY SCORE /10

MEDAL MOUNTAIN!

THIS FELLA HAS WON LOADS OF TROPHIES! USE THE MEDALS IN HIS COLLECTION TO GUESS WHO IT IS!

? 2 1 1

10 POINTS FOR CORRECT ANSWER

MY SCORE /10

SPOT THE SPIES!

SHARPEN UP YER EYES AND CIRCLE THE FIVE GAFFERS WATCHIN' PLAYERS IN THIS RAMMED FOOTY CROWD!

2 POINTS FOR EACH CORRECT ANSWER

MY SCORE /10

FOOTY FRIENDS!

CAN YOU NAME THE CLUB WHERE THIS PAIR BECAME MATES?

ANSWER

10 POINTS FOR CORRECT ANSWER

MY SCORE /10

TURNSTILE TOTALS!

MATCH THE PREM'S FIVE SMALLEST STADIUMS WITH THE NUMBER OF FANS THEY CAN FIT INSIDE!

1 CRAVEN COTTAGE

2 FRATTON PARK

3 THE MADEJSKI STADIUM

4 VICARAGE ROAD

5 THE JJB STADIUM

a 19,920

b 20,328

c 22,602

d 24,045

e 25,138

2 POINTS FOR EACH CORRECT ANSWER

MY SCORE /10

WORLD SUPERSTARS!

MATCH!

20

DECO
PORTUGAL

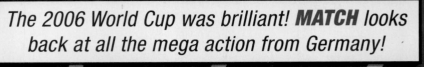

The 2006 World Cup was brilliant! **MATCH** looks back at all the mega action from Germany!

WHAT A WICKED

GREAT GOALS!

ESTEBAN CAMBIASO!

JOE COLE!

TORSTEN FRINGS!

There were some wicked World Cup goals, including Torsten Frings' rocket, Joe Cole's belter and Argentina's amazing 25-pass strike!

ROONEY ROARS BACK!

Rooney made an amazing recovery to be fit for the World Cup, and made his debut in the 2-0 win over Trinidad & Tobago!

WORLD CUP!

RECORD BREAKER RONALDO!

Big Ron broke the all-time World Cup scoring record when he bagged his 15th goal in finals after five minutes against Ghana! Good on ya!

BLINGIN' BOOTS!

From Ronaldinho's white and gold boots to Robben's flash Orange numbers and Becks' blue beauties, we saw some well wicked footwear!

WHAT A WICKED WORLD CUP!

CRAZY COACHES!

OTTO PFISTER!

LUIS ARAGONES!

GUUS HIDDINK!

Togo's Otto Pfister quit his job then came back, while Luis Aragones of Spain and Australia's Guus Hiddink were absolutely bonkers too!

GREAT GAMES!

ENGLAND 2
SWEDEN 2

ARGENTINA .. 2
MEXICO 1

McDonald's

ITALY 2
GERMANY 0

SPAIN 4
UKRAINE 0

Italy's semi-final win over Germany was a real cracker, but there were loads more wicked games that wowed fans at the World Cup!

CRAZY CELEBRATIONS!

Ivory Coast entertained us with their crazy group dance, Fernando Torres struck a wicked pose and there were loads more top celebrations!

WHAT A WICKED WORLD CUP!

RUBBISH REFS!

The refs sucked! Graham Poll booked a player three times, and the ref in charge of Holland against Portugal sent four players off! Madness!

FANTASTIC FREE-KICKS!

BECKHAM v ECUADOR!

SRNA v AUSTRALIA!

There were loads of wicked free-kick net-busters, but MATCH's fave was England skipper David Beckham's scorcher against Ecuador!

VAN PERSIE v IVORY COAST!

VILLA v UKRAINE!

SURPRISE STARS!

PHILIPP LAHM!

OMAR BRAVO!

MAXI RODRIGUEZ!

Loads of players burst on to the World Cup stage, like Germany's Philipp Lahm, Omar Bravo of Mexico and Maxi Rodriguez of Argentina!

FAB FANS!

The fans at the World Cup came to party, and they made it a fun footy festival with their bright colours, crazy outfits and cool dancing!

WHAT A WICKED WORLD CUP!

GOLDEN BOOT!

HERNAN CRESPO!

MIROSLAV KLOSE!

FERNANDO TORRES!

Germany's Miroslav Klose topped the goalscoring charts with five strikes, while Hernan Crespo and Fernando Torres rocked too!

SUPER STROPS!

Rooney threw his toys out of the pram when he was subbed against Sweden, while Cristiano Ronaldo blubbed when he went off injured!

TOUGH TACKLES!

As well as great goals and exciting action, there were loads of bone-crunchin' tackles! No-one wanted to lose, so the studs were up!

PREMIERSHIP STARS!

TOMAS ROSICKY!

ANDRIY SHEVCHENKO!

Germany 2006 gave us a glimpse of what to expect from stars like Shevchenko, Rosicky and Tevez before they came to the Prem!

CARLOS TEVEZ!

WHAT A WICKED WORLD CUP!

SLICK STADIUMS!

BERLIN!

DORTMUND!

MUNICH!

MATCH loved the wicked World Cup stadiums, like Munich's space-age Allianz Arena and the amazing Olympic stadium in Berlin!

SLAMMIN' SHOOT-OUTS!

Okay, so England crashed out in a shoot-out against Portugal, but Germany v Argentina and France v Italy in the final were well exciting!

WORLD CHAMPS ITALY!

Wicked defender Fabio Cannavaro lifted the World Cup for Italy after the Azzurri beat France 5-3 in a penalty shoot-out! Top stuff, dudes!

LA LIGA QUIZ!

MY SCORE /60

NEXT QUIZ PAGE 66

ANSWERS PAGE 92-93

GIANLUCA ZAMBROTTA QUIZ!

ZAMBROTTA'S ONE OF THE WORLD'S TOP DEFENDERS, BUT HOW MUCH DO YA KNOW ABOUT THE BARCELONA STAR?

1 Which country does the defender play for?

2 How old is Zambrotta – is he 26, 29 or 32?

3 From which club did Barça sign him back in the summer?

4 Which other player signed for Barca at exactly the same time as Zambrotta?

5 How many goals did he score at the 2006 World Cup – three, one or none?

2 POINTS FOR EACH CORRECT ANSWER

MY SCORE /10

NATIONAL DRESS!

THIS LA LIGA STAR IS DRESSED IN HIS COUNTRY'S TRADITIONAL GEAR! BUT CAN YOU TELL ME WHO IT IS?

ANSWER

10 POINTS FOR CORRECT ANSWER

MY SCORE /10

BADGE IT!

UNSCRAMBLE THIS BADGE AN' WRITE THE TEAM IT BELONGS TO!

10 POINTS FOR CORRECT ANSWER

MY SCORE /10

ANSWER

KINGS OF SPAIN!

WHO'S THE BEST CLUB IN SPAIN? MATCH THESE TEAMS WITH THE NUMBER OF LA LIGA TITLES THEY'VE LIFTED!

2 POINTS FOR EACH CORRECT ANSWER

MY SCORE /10

1 BARCELONA	2 DEPORTIVO	3 GETAFE	4 REAL MADRID	5 ATLETICO MADRID
a **29**	b **0**	c **18**	d **1**	e **9**

CROSSWORD!

WRITE THE ANSWERS, THEN REARRANGE THE LETTERS IN THE GOLD SQUARES TO REVEAL THE 'GOALDEN' WORD!

Unscramble the letters in the gold boxes to work out the 'Goalden' word!

GOALDEN ANSWER

ACROSS

1. Barcelona's stadium! (3,4)

4. Last season's Primera Liga top scorer, _____ Eto'o! (6)

6. Cesc Fabregas' old club! (9)

7. Real Madrid's nickname! (10)

8. Liverpool coach Rafa Benitez used to boss this club! (8)

9. Spain's No.1, Iker _____! (8)

DOWN

2. Getafe 'keeper Roberto Abbondanzieri plays for this country! (9)

3. Atletico and Real both play in this city! (6)

5. Valencia star who netted three World Cup goals! (5,5)

10. La Liga club, Celta _____! (4)

1/2 POINT FOR EACH CORRECT ANSWER + 5 FOR GOALDEN ANSWER

MY SCORE /10

BEHIND THE BULL!

WHICH WICKED LA LIGA MIDFIELDER IS HIDIN' BEHIND THIS CRAZY SPANISH BULL? HAVE A GUESS, SENOR!

> 1. I'm a hero at The Bernabeu!

> 2. I've got a famous wife!

> 3. I used to be the captain of my country!

10 POINTS FOR CORRECT ANSWER

MY SCORE /10

WORLD SUPERSTARS!

MATCH!

XABI ALONSO
SPAIN

JOE COLE'S

MATCH looks at the amazing career of the **CHELSEA** & **ENGLAND** star!

He's still only 24, but it seems like Joe Cole has been around forever! The wicked midfielder burst on to the scene in 1998 as an exciting 17-year-old for West Ham, and he's just got better and better. Whether it's great goals, wicked tricks, England caps or trophies - Joe's got it all! Check out his scrapbook!

MARCH 1998:
ENGLAND UNDER-16s!

Check out Joe showing off his silky skills for the England Under-16 team!

SEPTEMBER 1998:
YOUNG STAR!

Coley was mates with England boss Kevin Keegan when he was just a teenager!

JUNE 1998:
ENGLAND UNDER-18s!

The West Ham lad quickly moved through the England youth teams!

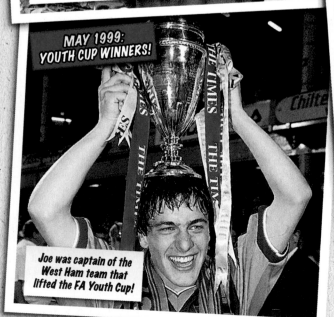

MAY 1999:
YOUTH CUP WINNERS!

Joe was captain of the West Ham team that lifted the FA Youth Cup!

SCRAPBOOK!

JANUARY 1999: WEST HAM DEBUT!

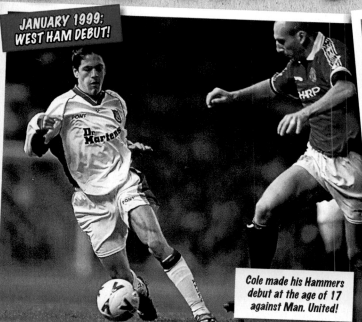

Cole made his Hammers debut at the age of 17 against Man. United!

JANUARY 2000: ENGLAND UNDER-21s!

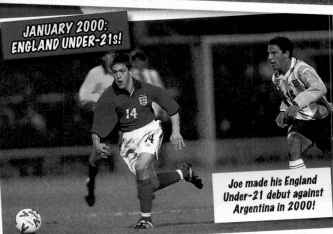

Joe made his England Under-21 debut against Argentina in 2000!

JANUARY 2000: MATCH AWARD!

MATCH is big mates with JC! Here he is with one of his awards!

APRIL 2000: COLE & CARRICK!

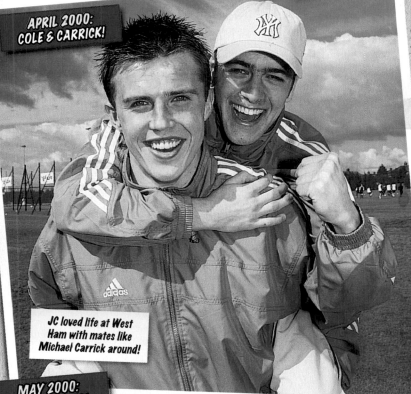

JC loved life at West Ham with mates like Michael Carrick around!

MAY 2000: LOOKING COOL!

Joe, in the middle, looked 'shady' at an Adidas event! He also worked with Coca-Cola at Wembley!

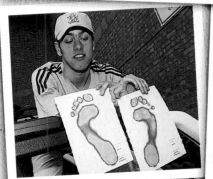

AUGUST 2002: HAMMERS CAPTAIN!

Hammers skipper at the age of just 20. Nice one, Coley!

FEBRUARY 2001: MORE AWARDS!

Joe bagged loads of MATCH awards for his wicked displays at West Ham!

APRIL 2001: DRIVING AMBITION!

The trickster loved to have a laugh with the MATCH cameras! Here he is pretending to drive the England team bus!

MARCH 2001: WRESTLE MANIA!

Tough man Cole arm-wrestled for a £50 bet on TV show Soccer AM!

CHECK OUT SOME OF JOE'S MAD HAIRCUTS!

MAY 2001: ENGLAND DEBUT!

The West Ham star made his England debut in the ace 4-0 friendly win against Mexico!

OCTOBER 2002: PRIME TIME!

Here's Joe and his girlfriend at Prime Minister Tony Blair's gaff. Nice one!

JUNE 2002: WORLD CUP DEBUT!

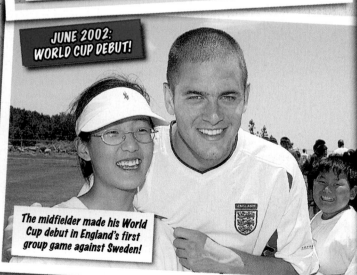

The midfielder made his World Cup debut in England's first group game against Sweden!

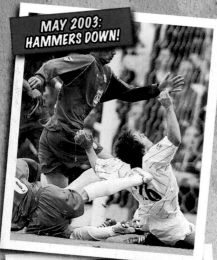

MAY 2003: HAMMERS DOWN!

JUNE 2003: FIRST ENGLAND GOAL!

Joe came off the bench in the friendly against Serbia-Montenegro to bag his first England goal with a free-kick!

COLE'S GOALS!

The Hammers' skipper was gutted when his team were relegated!

Arsenal 0-2 Chelsea
December 18, 2005

The Chelsea trickster gave Blues fans some Christmas cheer with a well-taken finish against Arsenal at Highbury!

Norwich 1-3 Chelsea
March 5, 2005

After giving the ball away, Coley worked hard to win it back, beat two defenders and cracked a beauty into the top corner!

J.COLE 10 **VERON 20**

AUGUST 2003: CHELSEA STAR!

Joe signed for Chelsea for £6.6 million at the same time as Juan Veron!

OCTOBER 2003: BENCH WARMER!

Despite his big move from West Ham, Joe struggled to get into Chelsea's team!

England 2-2 Sweden
June 20, 2006

At the 2006 World Cup, Cole chested the ball down and hit a sweet volley that flew past the Sweden 'keeper! Get in!

JULY 2004: EURO 2004 PAIN!

JULY 2004: CHELSEA ON TOUR!

Joe was in the squad for Euro 2004, but didn't play a game. Bad luck, mate!

Check out Joe and the Chelsea boys on a pre-season tour of the USA!

West Ham 5-4 Bradford
February 12, 2000

In a nine-goal thriller at Upton Park, Joe bagged his first Prem goal with a wicked strike after an amazing solo run!

**FEBRUARY 2005:
LEAGUE CUP KINGS!**

Joe picked up his first trophy as Chelsea beat Liverpool in the Carling Cup final!

**APRIL 2004:
EURO CRASH!**

Chelsea bombed out of the Champions League in the semis against Monaco!

**MAY 2005:
JUST CHAMPION!**

Joe and Damien Duff celebrated Chelsea's first title win in 50 years!

**MARCH 2005:
GOAL GRABBER!**

JC rocked for England in the World Cup qualifier against Northern Ireland!

**APRIL 2005:
MODEL PLAYER!**

Coley loved modelling the flash new England kit with Chelsea mate John Terry!

**MAY 2006:
WEMBLEY WAY!**

Joe and the England lads had a kick-about at the new Wembley Stadium!

APRIL 2006: PREM WINNER!

Joey bagged in Chelsea's 3-0 win over Man. United that sealed another title!

JUNE 2006: ROYAL CHIT-CHAT!

Coley had a natter with posh Prince William before the World Cup finals!

JUNE 2006: ENGLAND STAR!

Joe put in a Man Of The Match display in the 1-0 win over Paraguay!

JUNE 2006: GREAT GOAL!

The tricky winger bagged a 30-yard screamer in the 2-2 draw with Sweden!

JULY 2006: ENGLAND OUT!

JC was subbed as England crashed out of the World Cup against Portugal. Gutted!

JOE COLE: THE FUTURE!

What will the future hold for Joe? We dunno, but it's sure to be wicked!

Birmingham 2-3 West Ham
November 30, 1999

Joe Cole's first professional goal was well dramatic! He bagged a 90th-minute winner for West Ham in the League Cup!

Chelsea 3-1 Colchester
February 19, 2006

The England star scored two goals in this FA Cup clash, and his second was class – a 90th-minute curler into the top corner!

England 2-3 Denmark
November 16, 2003

After a clever move, Coley sidefooted Wayne Rooney's pass into the Denmark net! He took his shirt off in celebration!

Chelsea 3-0 Man. United
April 29, 2006

The midfielder beat Ferdinand and Vidic before coolly slotting past Van der Sar and sealing another title win for Chelsea!

PAUL'S PROBLEM!

Spurs 'keeper Paul Robinson is on the lookout!

Anyone seen my car keys?

DROP AND GIVE ME 20!

Chelsea's Arjen Robben gets extra press-ups at training!

1

THE WIFE'S GOT THESE, TOO!

DIAMOND EARRING!

It might be a bit girly, but it's good enough for Beckham!

2

TASTY GIRLFRIEND!

Every top player needs a pretty girl on his arm!

LOVE YOU, ASHLEY! KISS, KISS!

3

FOOTBALLERS' BLING!

To be a proper footy star, you've gotta have loads of cool stuff! Check out how you can be a bling player!

FLASH PAD!

Get yourself a mega house with a funky pool and big plasma TVs!

BLING BOOTS!

Ronaldinho has worn boots that cost £3,000 with real gold in 'em!

4

I DRIVE A DIFFERENT CAR EVERY DAY!

FAST CARS!

Footy stars love Ferraris and Porsches!

5

MATCH!

TOMAS ROSICKY
CZECH REPUBLIC

...WENT TO A CELEBRITY BASH!

"That would have been Ashley Cole's last birthday party, because there were quite a few celebrities there. It was a great night and I met a few new famous people, but I don't really go in for the celebrity stuff too much!"

...CRIED WITH LAUGHTER!

"The other day, when me and Robbie Keane were playing golf with two guys. We kept unclipping their golf bags from the buggies, so when they drove off their bags flew off the back! I had to dive into a sand bunker because I was laughing so hard!"

TOTTENHAM & ENGLAND midfielder JERMAINE JENAS has a laugh telling MATCH all about his cool footy life!

JERMAINE

...HAD THE MICKEY TAKEN!

"At the end of last season I went into training wearing some gear which the lads didn't take to. I liked it, but they thought it was a bit bright so they gave me loads of stick. Robbie Keane thinks he's a right joker, so he led the banter!"

...HIT ROW Z!

"That happened at the worst place last season - when I went back to St. James' Park to play Newcastle! After I hit the shot and saw it shooting to Row Z, I thought, 'God, why didn't I do this or that?' But you don't have time to think in a match!"

...PLAYED BEACH FOOTY!

"I had a really big game of beach footy a couple of summers ago! My friend Harvey, from So Solid Crew, had his stag do before he got married. We all went out to Puerto Banus in Marbella and had a great laugh - and a wicked game of football!"

JENAS
THE LAST TIME I...

...FELT REALLY PROUD!

"That normally happens after each game. I usually come off the pitch with some feeling of pride in what I've done. I go into most matches with a target of what I want to do, and if I've done that at the end, I'll feel proud!"

...SPLASHED OUT!

"That was probably when I went on a shopping spree to get some new gear. I go to a street called Brompton Road in South London, because there are a couple of shops down there I like. That's where I get most of my casual stuff from!"

...ATE SOMETHING UNHEALTHY!

"Last weekend! I eat healthily of course, but I'm lucky to be able to eat what I want because I don't put weight on easily. I can have fast food whenever I like, so I had a huge McDonald's last weekend and a Nando's chicken as well!"

...READ MATCH!

"It's always in our physio room at the training ground, so I read it all the time when I'm getting a massage. I remember reading about myself getting advice off Dr Footy. He said some good stuff, which I'm going to try to take this season!"

SERIE A QUIZ!

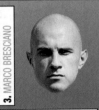

MY SCORE /60

NEXT QUIZ PAGE 70!

ANSWERS PAGE 92-93!

BADGE IT!

WHICH ITALIAN CLUB DOES THIS BADGE BELONG TO, DUDES?

PARM

A A.C.

10 POINTS FOR CORRECT ANSWER

MY SCORE /10

SERIE A SUPER SALES!

1. FABIO CANNAVARO — ANSWER

2. ANDRIY SHEVCHENKO — ANSWER

3. MARCO BRESCIANO — ANSWER

4. GIANLUCA ZAMBROTTA — ANSWER

5. FABIO GROSSO — ANSWER

ALL THIS FLASH TALENT WAS SOLD BY SERIE A CLUBS LAST SUMMER, BUT WHICH WICKED TEAMS DID THEY JOIN? WRITE THEM DOWN!

2 POINTS FOR EACH CORRECT ANSWER

MY SCORE /10

TRANSFER TRACKER!

CHRISTIAN VIERI'S PLAYED FOR LOADSA EUROPEAN TEAMS IN HIS CAREER, BUT WHICH TWO ITALIAN CLUBS ARE MISSING?

1995-1996	ATALANTA
1996-1997	JUVENTUS
1998-1999	? ?
1999-2005	? ?
2005-2006	AC MILAN

5 POINTS FOR EACH CORRECT ANSWER

MY SCORE /10

dream team!

I'VE PICKED ONE STAR-PACKED SERIE A SIDE HERE! CHECK MY CLUES TO SEE IF YOU CAN WORK THEM ALL OUT!

Former Italy No.1 – AP!

GK

Ex-Brazil captain at AC Milan! — RB

Roma & France defender – PM! — CB

Inter Milan's World Cup winner! — CB

Italy star like a fast car – MF! — LB — ANSWER

Fiorentina winger – SF! — RM

Inter Milan & Argentina rock! — CM

Roma's skilful captain! — CM

Chile's ex-Udinese star! — LM — David Pizarro!

AC Milan striker – AG! — S

Pippo Inzaghi's brother! — S — ANSWER

1 POINT FOR EACH CORRECT ANSWER

MY SCORE /10

SPOT THE DIFFERENCE!

SCAN THESE TWO SERIE A ACTION SHOTS AND CIRCLE THE FIVE DIFFERENCES!

2 POINTS FOR EACH CORRECT ANSWER

MY SCORE /10

STAR NAMES!

THREE SERIE A CLUBS CAN BE MADE FROM THIS NAME! FIND ONE FOR TEN POINTS!

ANSWER

10 POINTS FOR CORRECT ANSWER

MY SCORE /10

WORLD SUPERSTARS!

MICHAEL ESSIEN
GHANA

Midfield star **KIERAN RICHARDSON** tells **MATCH** what he gets up to on a **MAN. UNITED** matchday!

10.00am

WAKEY, WAKEY!

"If we're at home and kicking off at three o'clock, I'll get up at ten. I don't have breakfast at home because we have a pre-match meal at Old Trafford. I usually put some music on and watch Soccer AM or the news on TV!"

KIERAN RICHARDSON...
MAN. UNIT ED
MA

11.00am

DRIVE TIME!

"I leave my house at about eleven o'clock, and it takes 20 minutes to get to Old Trafford. I listen to R'n'B and hip-hop in the car. I'm not nervous at this point - you're excited because you want to get out there and play!"

11.30am

GREAT GRUB!

"We usually eat at around 11.30. It's a buffet thing, so you get a big selection. There are loads of pastas, potatoes, chicken, spaghetti bolognese, plus all sorts of vegetables and cereals. There's a massive choice!"

12.00pm

1.00pm

TEAM MEETING!

"The manager takes the team meeting at 1.00pm. It's the first time you find out who's in the team, so that keeps us on our toes. The gaffer likes it when we don't know who's starting, as we all have to be prepared!"

LOUNGE OUT!

"After the meal, we go downstairs to the lounge at Old Trafford and relax. Usually there's a midday game to watch on TV, but some people read the papers. We'll just chat and get ready for the team news."

ED'S TCHDAY!

2.20pm

WARMING UP!

"We go out on to the pitch and have a proper warm-up. We're put through our paces doing stretches and a little running, and then we'll get the balls out and do our own thing. It's really important to warm up properly!"

2.50pm

CRAZY TIME!

"We'll come back in at about 2.50pm and the dressing room is hectic, because everyone's rushing around getting ready! The gaffer says his final words, then we go out there and hopefully do the business!"

CHILLING OUT!

"I always watch Match Of The Day because I like to see what else has happened in the Premiership. Sometimes I'll go out for a meal with friends, but you usually just want to chill out after a hard week training!"

5.00pm

GAME OVER!

"If we win the game then everyone's happy afterwards! If we lose, it's very quiet in the dressing room. Sometimes you'll speak to the press and the media after the game, and you don't mind if you've won!"

10.30pm

FREDDY ADU QUIZ!

THE A-DUDE IS THE HOTTEST TALENT IN THE USA! SHOW WHAT YA KNOW 'BOUT HIM BY ANSWERIN' THESE FIVE QUESTIONS!

1 How old is Freddy – is he 16, 17 or 18?

2 Which Major League Soccer club does the striker play for?

3 True or False? Adu's nickname is 'Bullet Boy' because of his speed on the pitch.

4 He plays for the USA, but in which African country was he born?

5 Which sportswear giant sponsors the super striker?

2 POINTS FOR EACH CORRECT ANSWER | MY SCORE /10

CRUNCH TIME!

MATCH THE RIVAL TEAMS FROM JAPAN, HOLLAND, BRAZIL, GERMANY AND AUSTRALIA!

2 POINTS FOR EACH CORRECT ANSWER

MY SCORE /10

1 SANTOS	2 FEYENOORD	3 JUBILO IWATA	4 1860	5 NEWCASTLE

A BAYERN MUNICH	B CORINTHIANS	C AJAX	D CENTRAL COAST	E SHIMIZU S-PULSE

DR. FOOTY'S FACTS & FIB!

READ MY THREE FACTS ABOUT WORLD FOOTY AND THEN PUT A CROSS BY THE FALSE ONE!

1. Games that are drawn in Chile's National Cup are decided by three-a-side extra-time! ☐

2. South America's version of the Champions League is called The Copa Libertadores! ☐

3. Famous Greek club AEK Athens are nicknamed 'The Belly Dancers'! ☐

10 POINTS FOR CORRECT ANSWER | MY SCORE /10

ARGEN-TEAM-A!

FIVE OF THESE TEAMS PLAY IN THE ROCK-HARD ARGENTINIAN LEAGUE. STICK A TICK BY ALL FIVE OF THEM!

✓ INDEPENDIENTE	✓ DEPORTIVO SAPRISSA
✓ BOCA JUNIORS	✓ WALSALL
✓ RIVER PLATE	✓ NEWELL'S OLD BOYS
✓ ESTUDIANTES	✓ ALAVES

2 POINTS FOR EACH CORRECT ANSWER | MY SCORE /10

WORDFIT!

THERE ARE 20 WORLD STARS HERE! FIT THEM IN THE GRID TO BAG MAX POINTS. MAKE SURE YOU USE A PENCIL, THOUGH!

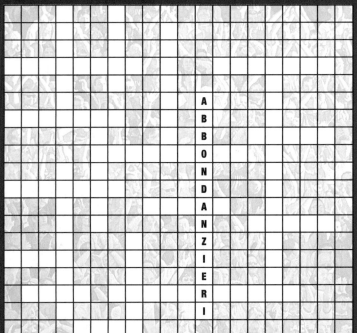

>> ABBONDANZIERI
>> BEASLEY
>> BOUMNIJEL
>> DELGADO
>> DONOVAN
>> EDMAN
>> FRED
>> FREI
>> GALASEK
>> KOLLER
>> KONE
>> LINDEROTH
>> MALOUDA
>> POBORSKY
>> RIVALDO
>> SCHWEINSTEIGER
>> TEVEZ
>> VAN DER VAART
>> VERON
>> WANCHOPE
>> YORKE

1/2 POINT FOR EACH CORRECT ANSWER | MY SCORE /10

HEAD OF TWO HALVES!

ANSWER

WHICH TWO FRENCH LEAGUE STARS HAVE BEEN STUCK TOGETHER HERE? HAVE A GO!

ANSWER

5 POINTS FOR EACH CORRECT ANSWER | MY SCORE /10

WORLD SUPERSTARS!

MATCH!

ARJEN ROBBEN
HOLLAND

MY BEST FO

Ever wondered which footy players are best friends and what they have in common? **MATCH** asks the stars who their top mates are!

TIM CAHILL
EVERTON

"Me and Archie Thompson – who used to be at PSV – are very close friends. He's a legend and the reason why I punch the corner flag after I score! I only really get the chance to see him when we're both with Australia!"

ASHLEY YOUNG
WATFORD

"Marlon King is my best mate in footy! We're alike as characters, but we're similar on the pitch as well. We like the same films, we eat together, go round each other's houses and we both like R'n'B and hip-hop!"

NIGEL REO-COKER
WEST HAM

"My best mates in football are Anton Ferdinand, Malvin Kamara and Wade Small! We played together when we were young, and I was with Malvin and Wade at MK Dons before I moved to West Ham in 2004!"

OTY MATE!

GARY NEVILLE
MAN. UNITED

"My best mates are my brother Phil and David Beckham! I've been lucky to have a few good mates over the years, such as Nicky Butt and Scholesy. Now I spend most of my time with Phil or Becks!"

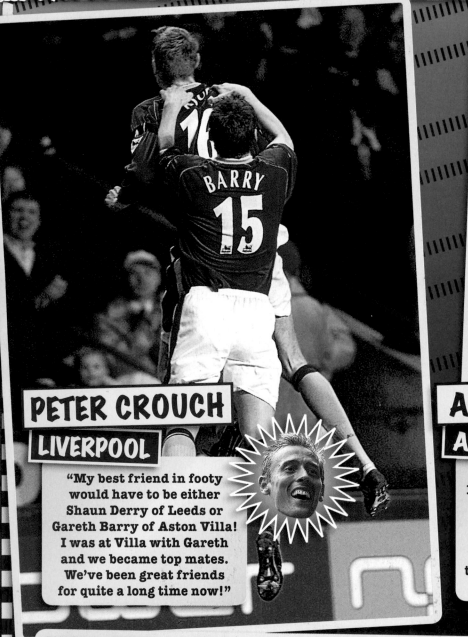

PETER CROUCH
LIVERPOOL

"My best friend in footy would have to be either Shaun Derry of Leeds or Gareth Barry of Aston Villa! I was at Villa with Gareth and we became top mates. We've been great friends for quite a long time now!"

ALEXANDER HLEB
ARSENAL

"My best mate is Cesc Fabregas, and I get on really well with Mathieu Flamini and Robin van Persie too. Having good friends at Arsenal has really helped the way we play – and helped me settle in at the club!"

KIERAN RICHARDSON
MAN. UNITED

"My best mate in footy is probably Darren Bent. I've got a lot of friends at United, but outside the club I get on well with Benty. We played against each other a lot when we were younger, and then together for the under-21s!"

LEROY LITA
READING

"I have a few good mates, but Liam Rosenior of Fulham is probably the best! I've known him for about four or five years now, because we played together at Bristol City. We still see each other a lot!"

CHARLES N'ZOGBIA
NEWCASTLE

"Jean Alain Boumsong is a big friend of mine because he speaks French, like me. When he was at Newcastle we got on well because we have a lot in common. He was like my big brother and always helped me!"

JIMMY BULLARD
FULHAM

"Me and Mike Pollitt, the Wigan goalkeeper, are good mates. Polli is a right laugh because he's bonkers – he's worse than me! We went on holiday together and had a great time!"

LIAM RIDGEWELL
ASTON VILLA

"My best friend in football is my Aston Villa team-mate Steven Davis! We first met in Villa's youth team and we've been friends ever since. We came through the youth ranks together and he's a top man!"

FOOTBALL LEAGUE QUIZ!

MY SCORE /60

ANSWERS PAGE 92-93

ENGLAND YOUNG GUNS!

 1 BEN WATSON
 2 NATHAN DYER
 3 CAMERON JEROME
 4 BILLY JONES
 5 RICHARD CHAPLOW

 HERE ARE FIVE HOT PROSPECTS FROM THE FOOTY LEAGUE! MATCH THEM UP TO THEIR CLUB – IT'S WELL EASY!

ENGLAND ENGLAND ENGLAND ENGLAND

a CREWE ALEXANDRA FOOTBALL CLUB — CREWE
b SOUTHAMPTON FC — SOUTHAMPTON
c CRYSTAL PALACE — CRYSTAL PALACE
d BIRMINGHAM CITY FOOTBALL CLUB — BIRMINGHAM
e — WEST BROM

2 POINTS FOR EACH CORRECT ANSWER

MY SCORE /10

PERCY'S PLAYERS!

WHO'S THIS BLINGED-UP CHAMPIONSHIP STRIKER? WHAT HE'S DOING IN THE PICTURE IS A BIG CLUE, MATCH FANS!

ANSWER

10 POINTS FOR CORRECT ANSWER

MY SCORE /10

GROUNDED!

CAN YOU NAME THE WICKED CHAMPIONSHIP CLUB THAT PLAY AT THIS BLOCKBUSTIN' MEGA NEW STADIUM IN THE MIDLANDS?

ANSWER

10 POINTS FOR CORRECT ANSWER

MY SCORE /10

SPOT THE BALL!

SUNDERLAND ACE DEAN WHITEHEAD IS GOING FOR GOAL, BUT WOT SQUARE IS THE BALL IN?

1 2 3 4 5

A B C D E F G H I

10 POINTS FOR CORRECT ANSWER

MY SCORE /10

LEAGUE OF NATIONS!

THIS LOT PLAY IN THE CHAMPIONSHIP, BUT THEY AIN'T ENGLISH! LINK 'EM UP WITH THE COUNTRY THEY'RE FROM!

ROBERT EARNSHAW NORWICH — A. NORTHERN IRELAND
MIKAEL FORSSELL BIRMINGHAM — B. BELGIUM
GRZEGORZ RASIAK SOUTHAMPTON — C. FINLAND
DAVID HEALY LEEDS — D. WALES
CARL HOEFKENS STOKE — E. POLAND

2 POINTS FOR EACH CORRECT ANSWER

MY SCORE /10

MATCH-UP!

ALL YA GOTTA DO IS MATCH THE STADIUM AN' FOOTY BADGES TO THE CLUB THEY BELONG TO! JOIN 'EM ALL UP FOR TEN TOP POINTS!

 A ELLAND ROAD
 B ASHTON GATE
 C BRUNTON PARK
 D RICOH ARENA
 E STADIUM OF LIGHT

1 SUNDERLAND
2 LEEDS
3 CARLISLE
4 BRISTOL CITY
5 COVENTRY

 V
 W
 X
 Y
 Z CARLISLE UNITED

1 POINT FOR EACH CORRECT ANSWER

MY SCORE /10

WORLD SUPERSTARS!

MATCH!

LIONEL MESSI
ARGENTINA

PREMIERSHIP PLAYERS OF THE SEASON!

Using the special MATCHfacts ratings for every Premiership game, **MATCH** looks back at the top players last season!

ARSENAL!

THIERRY HENRY — 1
✪ AGE: 29 ✪ POSITION: STRIKER

LOWDOWN! Henry was Arsenal's best player in 2005-06 – and the best in the Premiership too! The France striker scored 27 goals, with eight assists and 11 Star Ratings. The Gunners fans love their super skipper!

PLAYED	32	STARS	11	AVE. RATING	7.25

JOSE REYES — 2
✪ AGE: 25 ✪ POSITION: STRIKER

LOWDOWN! Reyes only scored five Prem goals last season, but his displays were always good. Arsenal used him as a striker as well as on the left wing, and the speedy Spaniard always did the business!

PLAYED	26	STARS	2	AVE. RATING	7.15

SOL CAMPBELL — 3
✪ AGE: 32 ✪ POSITION: DEFENDER

LOWDOWN! Injury meant Campbell only played 20 league games, but he showed his quality when called on. The centre-back missed two months between February and April before returning for a strong finish!

PLAYED	20	STARS	2	AVE. RATING	6.80

KOLO TOURE — 4
✪ AGE: 25 ✪ POSITION: DEFENDER

LOWDOWN! Toure was in superb form in the centre of Arsenal's defence, and seemed to enjoy playing with young partner Philippe Senderos. The Ivory Coast star quickly became The Gunners' most important defender!

PLAYED	33	STARS	1	AVE. RATING	6.76

CESC FABREGAS — 5
✪ AGE: 19 ✪ POSITION: MIDFIELDER

LOWDOWN! Cesc was unbelievable in midfield for The Gunners, stepping into Patrick Vieira's big boots! The Spain playmaker showed his energy, skills and class, plus he bagged three Premiership goals! Fabregas was fab!

PLAYED	35	STARS	2	AVE. RATING	6.66

ASTON VILLA!

GAVIN McCANN — 1
✪ AGE: 28 ✪ POSITION: MIDFIELDER

LOWDOWN! Tough-tackling McCann was a strong force in Villa's midfield, and his eight yellow cards showed that! He only scored once, but that goal came against Newcastle – and the former Sunderland star loved it!

PLAYED	32	STARS	2	AVE. RATING	6.81

JAMES MILNER — 2
✪ AGE: 20 ✪ POSITION: MIDFIELDER

LOWDOWN! Milner joined Villa on loan from Newcastle, and made an instant impact with a goal against Spurs on his home debut! He played 27 Premiership games, chipping in with nine assists – and 150 crosses! Wow!

PLAYED	27	STARS	5	AVE. RATING	6.70

KEVIN PHILLIPS — 3
✪ AGE: 33 ✪ POSITION: STRIKER

LOWDOWN! Phillips found goals hard to come by in his only season at Villa Park, but he'll remember the winner he scored against local rivals Birmingham! He also bagged at former club Sunderland in November!

PLAYED	23	STARS	1	AVE. RATING	6.70

THOMAS SORENSEN — 4
✪ AGE: 30 ✪ POSITION: GOALKEEPER

LOWDOWN! The Denmark ace fought off the challenge from Stuart Taylor to stay as Villa's No.1, and only missed two league games. He kept 11 clean sheets, including two in derbies against Birmingham and West Brom!

PLAYED	36	STARS	0	AVE. RATING	6.64

LIAM RIDGEWELL — 5
✪ AGE: 22 ✪ POSITION: DEFENDER

LOWDOWN! Ridgewell coped well in his first full campaign in the Premiership, despite a nervous start. He finished with five goals – a good total for a centre-back – and won a new deal at the end of the season!

PLAYED	32	STARS	0	AVE. RATING	6.56

BIRMINGHAM!

MATTHEW UPSON

⊕ AGE: 27 ⊕ POSITION: DEFENDER

LOWDOWN! Upson's season ended in February due to injury, and Birmingham missed his cool head at the back so much they ended up being relegated! He made 33 clearances in his 24 games, and scored one goal!

| PLAYED | 24 | STARS | 4 | AVE. RATING | 6.46 |

MAIK TAYLOR 2

⊕ AGE: 35 ⊕ POSITION: GOALKEEPER

LOWDOWN! Taylor had a tough time last season as the last line in The Blues' defence, but he was a solid performer who only missed four games. His worst match came in the FA Cup in March, when Liverpool won 7-0. Doh!

| PLAYED | 34 | STARS | 3 | AVE. RATING | 6.26 |

MARTIN TAYLOR 3

⊕ AGE: 26 ⊕ POSITION: DEFENDER

LOWDOWN! The giant centre-back played more games than he might have expected because of Upson's injury, and did a sound job. His personal highlight was the 2-1 win over former club Blackburn in April.

| PLAYED | 21 | STARS | 0 | AVE. RATING | 6.14 |

JERMAINE PENNANT 4

⊕ AGE: 23 ⊕ POSITION: MIDFIELDER

LOWDOWN! JP didn't miss a game all season, and was always a threat on Birmingham's right wing. The former Arsenal wide man delivered 226 crosses, made five assists, and chipped in with two goals as well!

| PLAYED | 38 | STARS | 2 | AVE. RATING | 6.13 |

EMILE HESKEY 5

⊕ AGE: 28 ⊕ POSITION: STRIKER

LOWDOWN! Heskey started the season on fire with two goals in a 3-2 win over West Brom, but he slowed down after that, adding just two more. From 34 games, the big man needed to be more dangerous in front of goal!

| PLAYED | 34 | STARS | 1 | AVE. RATING | 6.00 |

BLACKBURN!

LUCAS NEILL

⊕ AGE: 28 ⊕ POSITION: DEFENDER

LOWDOWN! The Australia defender was at his tough-tackling best for Rovers, though his aggressive style earned him one red card and 12 yellows! Neill scored once in the league – in the 4-3 home win over Man. United!

| PLAYED | 35 | STARS | 2 | AVE. RATING | 6.69 |

TUGAY 2

⊕ AGE: 36 ⊕ POSITION: MIDFIELDER

LOWDOWN! Tugay is now 36, but he was class for Blackburn with his tidy passing and experience. He started the season on a high with a goal against Fulham, but finished it on a low with a red card against Man. City!

| PLAYED | 27 | STARS | 3 | AVE. RATING | 6.63 |

STEVEN REID 3

⊕ AGE: 25 ⊕ POSITION: MIDFIELDER

LOWDOWN! Reid switched from winger to central midfielder with brilliant results! His power and strong running impressed, and one of his four league goals, a long-range strike at Wigan, was an absolute cracker!

| PLAYED | 34 | STARS | 4 | AVE. RATING | 6.62 |

BRAD FRIEDEL 4

⊕ AGE: 35 ⊕ POSITION: GOALKEEPER

LOWDOWN! Big Brad was on top form last season, playing every league game. The USA star is an old dude, but seems to be getting better and better with age! He boasted an excellent record of 16 clean sheets.

| PLAYED | 38 | STARS | 1 | AVE. RATING | 6.55 |

MORTEN GAMST PEDERSEN 5

⊕ AGE: 25 ⊕ POSITION: MIDFIELDER

LOWDOWN! With nine goals and seven assists, Pedersen was one of Blackburn's most effective attacking players. The left-winger scored vital goals, including two against Man. United and the winner over Arsenal at home!

| PLAYED | 34 | STARS | 2 | AVE. RATING | 6.53 |

BOLTON!

TAL BEN HAIM
⚙ AGE: 24 ⚙ POSITION: DEFENDER

LOWDOWN! Ben Haim has been ace since joining Bolton on a free, and he was rock-solid at the back last season. The Israel centre-back was Bolton's star player four times, but did pick up eight yellow and one red card!

| PLAYED | 35 | STARS | 4 | AVE. RATING | 6.74 |

JUSSI JAASKELAINEN 2
⚙ AGE: 31 ⚙ POSITION: GOALKEEPER

LOWDOWN! The Finland 'keeper has been one of the best in the Premiership for a few years now, and was in fine form again as Bolton just missed out on a UEFA Cup spot. JJ played in all 38 league games too!

| PLAYED | 38 | STARS | 1 | AVE. RATING | 6.63 |

KEVIN DAVIES 3
⚙ AGE: 29 ⚙ POSITION: STRIKER

LOWDOWN! Davies struggled early on, scoring just two goals before Christmas, but he finished the campaign strongly. He scored against Newcastle, Sunderland, Man. United and then bagged two against Charlton!

| PLAYED | 37 | STARS | 4 | AVE. RATING | 6.59 |

RICARDO GARDNER 4
⚙ AGE: 28 ⚙ POSITION: DEFENDER

LOWDOWN! The Jamaican has been transformed since moving from left-wing to left-back, and is now one of the Premiership's best in his new position. He's quick, excellent going forward and a tough tackler, too!

| PLAYED | 30 | STARS | 4 | AVE. RATING | 6.53 |

BRUNO N'GOTTY 5
⚙ AGE: 35 ⚙ POSITION: DEFENDER

LOWDOWN! Even at 35, the French centre-back was a rock in defence for Bolton last season. His personal highlight happened outside the league, when he scored against Seville in the UEFA Cup group stage!

| PLAYED | 29 | STARS | 2 | AVE. RATING | 6.52 |

CHARLTON!

LUKE YOUNG
⚙ AGE: 27 ⚙ POSITION: DEFENDER

LOWDOWN! What a brilliant season for Young! The right-back missed only a few games and he was rewarded when he played in England's World Cup qualifiers against Wales, Northern Ireland, Austria and Poland!

| PLAYED | 32 | STARS | 1 | AVE. RATING | 6.36 |

HERMANN HREIDARSSON 2
⚙ AGE: 32 ⚙ POSITION: DEFENDER

LOWDOWN! The Iceland defender was a regular in Charlton's back four, doing a superb job at both centre-back and left-back. Hreidarsson made 73 blocks during the season, and was Charlton's star player twice!

| PLAYED | 34 | STARS | 2 | AVE. RATING | 6.34 |

JEROME THOMAS 3
⚙ AGE: 23 ⚙ POSITION: MIDFIELDER

LOWDOWN! Thomas is a lively winger who's at his best running with the ball. The ex-Arsenal trainee played in 25 games and made 16 starts. He scored once, in a 3-1 defeat away at Tottenham, and set up two goals!

| PLAYED | 25 | STARS | 0 | AVE. RATING | 6.28 |

DARREN BENT 4
⚙ AGE: 22 ⚙ POSITION: STRIKER

LOWDOWN! Bent was pure class for Charlton in his first season at the club! He kicked off with two goals against Sunderland and kept up a good goalscoring record, finally finishing with 18 in 36 games!

| PLAYED | 36 | STARS | 2 | AVE. RATING | 6.22 |

CHRIS PERRY 5
⚙ AGE: 33 ⚙ POSITION: DEFENDER

LOWDOWN! Veteran defender Perry played 28 league games for Charlton, scoring once – in the 3-0 win at Boro. He made 52 clearances and 16 blocks, and it was a surprise when he was released in the summer.

| PLAYED | 28 | STARS | 0 | AVE. RATING | 6.18 |

CHELSEA!

FRANK LAMPARD

⚙ **AGE:** 28 ⚙ **POSITION:** MIDFIELDER

LOWDOWN! Not many midfielders in the world can match up to Lamps, who boasted 16 goals and 11 Star Ratings from his 35 Premiership games. The England hero also provided nine assists and had 64 shots on target!

PLAYED	35	STARS	11	AVE. RATING	7.14

JOHN TERRY — 2

⚙ **AGE:** 25 ⚙ **POSITION:** DEFENDER

LOWDOWN! Chelsea's captain was at his very best as The Blues won their second title on the trot! JT missed only two games, and notched four league goals – including two winning strikes in 1-0 wins!

PLAYED	36	STARS	2	AVE. RATING	6.86

CLAUDE MAKELELE — 3

⚙ **AGE:** 33 ⚙ **POSITION:** MIDFIELDER

LOWDOWN! Makelele's not spectacular, but he does a steady job in midfield as the holding player. He didn't have a single shot on target and was booked seven times in the league, but Maka was still vital for Chelsea!

PLAYED	31	STARS	1	AVE. RATING	6.65

RICARDO CARVALHO — 4

⚙ **AGE:** 28 ⚙ **POSITION:** DEFENDER

LOWDOWN! Ricardo Carvalho wasn't always a regular, but when he played, he played well! The Portugal defender made 22 clearances, scored one goal and was sent off once too, against Charlton in January.

PLAYED	24	STARS	0	AVE. RATING	6.62

WILLIAM GALLAS — 5

⚙ **AGE:** 29 ⚙ **POSITION:** DEFENDER

LOWDOWN! Though he was often used at left-back, Gallas is best at centre-back and was in great form for Chelsea. The Frenchman scored five league goals, including a 90th-minute wonder strike to sink Tottenham!

PLAYED	34	STARS	2	AVE. RATING	6.50

EVERTON!

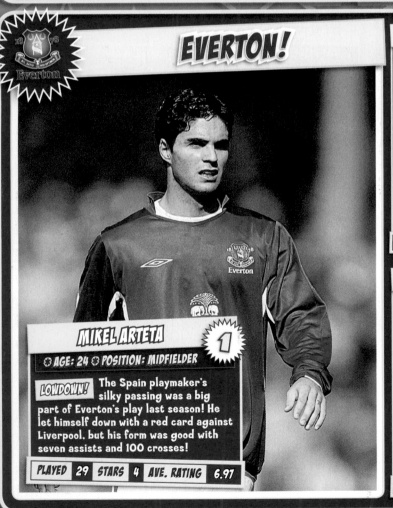

MIKEL ARTETA

⚙ **AGE:** 24 ⚙ **POSITION:** MIDFIELDER

LOWDOWN! The Spain playmaker's silky passing was a big part of Everton's play last season! He let himself down with a red card against Liverpool, but his form was good with seven assists and 100 crosses!

PLAYED	29	STARS	4	AVE. RATING	6.97

ALAN STUBBS — 2

⚙ **AGE:** 34 ⚙ **POSITION:** DEFENDER

LOWDOWN! Stubbs rejoined Everton from Sunderland midway through the season and made an instant impact. His experience was a big boost to The Toffees as the team began to move away from the relegation zone!

PLAYED	24	STARS	2	AVE. RATING	6.46

DAVID WEIR — 3

⚙ **AGE:** 36 ⚙ **POSITION:** DEFENDER

LOWDOWN! Another golden oldie centre-back for Everton. Weir missed just five games and linked up well with Stubbs again. The Scotland defender chipped in with one goal, the winner against Man. City at Goodison!

PLAYED	33	STARS	0	AVE. RATING	6.36

PHIL NEVILLE — 4

⚙ **AGE:** 29 ⚙ **POSITION:** DEFENDER

LOWDOWN! Neville was rarely out of the action in his first year at Goodison Park, playing as a defensive midfielder or right-back! He clocked up 12 bookings and two red cards – one in the derby defeat against Liverpool.

PLAYED	34	STARS	1	AVE. RATING	6.35

NIGEL MARTYN — 5

⚙ **AGE:** 40 ⚙ **POSITION:** GOALKEEPER

LOWDOWN! Martyn held off Richard Wright to retain the No.1 spot at Everton, but the ex-England 'keeper's season finished in January. A stress fracture to his ankle kept him sidelined and forced him to retire.

PLAYED	20	STARS	0	AVE. RATING	6.35

FULHAM!

STEED MALBRANQUE ✪ 1
⊙ AGE: 26 ⊙ POSITION: MIDFIELDER

LOWDOWN! Malbranque showed his class in Fulham's midfield, where his silky skills saw him hit six goals and pick up three assists. He finished the season strongly with three goals in his last six Premiership games.

PLAYED	34	STARS	3	AVE. RATING	6.20

MORITZ VOLZ ✪ 2
⊙ AGE: 23 ⊙ POSITION: DEFENDER

LOWDOWN! Volzy didn't play as many games as he would have liked in 2005-06, but his form at right-back was good enough to make him Fulham's second-best player! At 23, his game will get better and better.

PLAYED	23	STARS	0	AVE. RATING	6.09

LUIS BOA MORTE ✪ 3
⊙ AGE: 29 ⊙ POSITION: STRIKER

LOWDOWN! Boa Morte was one of Fulham's most exciting players last season with six goals, nine assists and 73 crosses! He's at his best with the ball out wide, but ten yellow cards and one red shows a bad temper!

PLAYED	35	STARS	5	AVE. RATING	5.97

PAPA BOUBA DIOP ✪ 4
⊙ AGE: 28 ⊙ POSITION: MIDFIELDER

LOWDOWN! The powerful midfielder is hard to stop on top form, so it was a shame for Fulham that Diop missed nearly half the season. The Senegal star scored twice, including the winning goal against Blackburn!

PLAYED	22	STARS	2	AVE. RATING	5.96

COLLINS JOHN ✪ 5
⊙ AGE: 20 ⊙ POSITION: STRIKER

LOWDOWN! John hit 11 league goals from just 16 starts, with 19 appearances from the bench. He scored two goals against Liverpool and one against Man. United, but his best was a wicked volley at Middlesbrough!

PLAYED	35	STARS	1	AVE. RATING	5.83

LIVERPOOL!

JAMIE CARRAGHER ✪ 1
⊙ AGE: 28 ⊙ POSITION: DEFENDER

LOWDOWN! Carragher is one of the best defenders in the Premiership, and just did enough to edge England team-mate Gerrard out of top spot. With 69 clearances and 12 blocks, Carra was a rock at the back!

PLAYED	36	STARS	4	AVE. RATING	7.14

STEVEN GERRARD ✪ 2
⊙ AGE: 26 ⊙ POSITION: MIDFIELDER

LOWDOWN! Stevie G was in terrific form, scoring ten league goals as well as being a top provider – he chipped in with five assists and 143 crosses. The midfielder also picked up the PFA Player Of The Year award!

PLAYED	32	STARS	6	AVE. RATING	7.12

SAMI HYYPIA ✪ 3
⊙ AGE: 32 ⊙ POSITION: DEFENDER

LOWDOWN! Hyypia's place came under threat from new signing Daniel Agger, but the Finn remained a regular and missed just two games. His partnership with Jamie Carragher was again one of the best in the league.

PLAYED	36	STARS	2	AVE. RATING	7.08

XABI ALONSO ✪ 4
⊙ AGE: 24 ⊙ POSITION: MIDFIELDER

LOWDOWN! Liverpool's Spain ace was a classy performer in the centre of midfield for The Reds, making 41 crosses and six assists. He scored three league goals, and picked up an impressive six Star Ratings too!

PLAYED	35	STARS	6	AVE. RATING	6.91

PEPE REINA ✪ 5
⊙ AGE: 24 ⊙ POSITION: GOALKEEPER

LOWDOWN! Reina can be well pleased with his first season in the Premiership! The Spain international kept 20 clean sheets in his 33 league games, which was excellent. He was harshly sent off at Chelsea in February.

PLAYED	33	STARS	1	AVE. RATING	6.91

MANCHESTER CITY!

JOEY BARTON 1
⦿ AGE: 24 ⦿ POSITION: MIDFIELDER

LOWDOWN! City's explosive midfielder had an action-packed year with six goals, six assists, ten yellow cards and one red! A tough tackler who can score from distance, Barton was City's most talked-about player!

PLAYED	31	STARS	5	AVE. RATING	6.97

SYLVAIN DISTIN 2
⦿ AGE: 28 ⦿ POSITION: DEFENDER

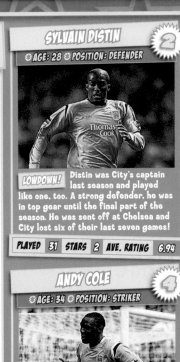

LOWDOWN! Distin was City's captain last season and played like one, too. A strong defender, he was in top gear until the final part of the season. He was sent off at Chelsea and City lost six of their last seven games!

PLAYED	31	STARS	2	AVE. RATING	6.94

RICHARD DUNNE 3
⦿ AGE: 27 ⦿ POSITION: DEFENDER

LOWDOWN! Distin's centre-back partner was also pretty solid for City last season! Dunne made 72 clearances and 19 blocks, and added three league goals. He was booked nine times though, which was a bit naughty!

PLAYED	32	STARS	0	AVE. RATING	6.69

ANDY COLE 4
⦿ AGE: 34 ⦿ POSITION: STRIKER

LOWDOWN! Cole made a great start to his City career, scoring nine goals in 22 games, before injury struck in February. But by then, the striker had shown his expert finishing and put in some fine performances.

PLAYED	22	STARS	1	AVE. RATING	6.68

DAVID JAMES 5
⦿ AGE: 36 ⦿ POSITION: GOALKEEPER

LOWDOWN! Jamo turned 36 in the summer, but is still one of England's best 'keepers! He played all 38 Premiership games and his form was good enough to claim a place in England's 2006 World Cup squad.

PLAYED	38	STARS	1	AVE. RATING	6.50

MANCHESTER UNITED!

PAUL SCHOLES 1
⦿ AGE: 31 ⦿ POSITION: MIDFIELDER

LOWDOWN! Despite an injury which meant he only played 20 games, Scholes still did enough to be United's top player. He scored twice, against Portsmouth and West Brom, and also picked up three assists.

PLAYED	20	STARS	3	AVE. RATING	6.95

WAYNE ROONEY 2
⦿ AGE: 20 ⦿ POSITION: STRIKER

LOWDOWN! With 16 goals, eight Star Man ratings and nine assists, Rooney had a super season at Old Trafford! A foot injury finished his season early, but not before he thrilled fans with displays of power and skill!

PLAYED	36	STARS	8	AVE. RATING	6.94

EDWIN VAN DER SAR 3
⦿ AGE: 35 ⦿ POSITION: GOALKEEPER

LOWDOWN! What a signing Van der Sar was! Snapped up from Fulham, his experience between the sticks gave United's defence a more solid look. He played all 38 league games and rarely made a mistake.

PLAYED	38	STARS	0	AVE. RATING	6.45

CRISTIANO RONALDO 4
⦿ AGE: 21 ⦿ POSITION: MIDFIELDER

LOWDOWN! The Portugal winger was in the zone last season! He produced 117 crosses, six assists and scored nine league goals, including three 'doubles'. A red card in the 3-1 defeat to Man. City was his low point.

PLAYED	33	STARS	3	AVE. RATING	6.45

RUUD VAN NISTELROOY 5
⦿ AGE: 30 ⦿ POSITION: STRIKER

LOWDOWN! The big Dutchman was his usual goal-poaching self, bagging 21 league goals in 28 starts – an excellent record. Towards the end of the season, he had to battle for a starting place with Louis Saha.

PLAYED	35	STARS	1	AVE. RATING	6.43

MIDDLESBROUGH!

CHRIS RIGGOTT ⭐1
⚽ AGE: 26 ⚽ POSITION: DEFENDER

LOWDOWN! Riggott had a top season for Boro, often partnering Gareth Southgate with Ugo Ehiogu out injured. His high point was scoring in the amazing 4-2 UEFA Cup semi-final second-leg win over Steaua Bucharest!

PLAYED	22	STARS	1	AVE. RATING	6.68

GEORGE BOATENG ⭐2
⚽ AGE: 31 ⚽ POSITION: MIDFIELDER

LOWDOWN! Rock-hard midfielder Boateng was crucial to Boro last season, so it's a shame he missed two months through injury. His return helped Boro move up the table and reach the UEFA Cup final.

PLAYED	26	STARS	1	AVE. RATING	6.58

GARETH SOUTHGATE ⭐3
⚽ AGE: 36 ⚽ POSITION: DEFENDER

LOWDOWN! Troubled by injuries, Southgate still showed his class in 24 appearances. Gaz's finest hour was guiding Boro to the UEFA Cup final, and at the end of the season he was named the club's new manager!

PLAYED	24	STARS	0	AVE. RATING	6.46

FABIO ROCHEMBACK ⭐4
⚽ AGE: 24 ⚽ POSITION: MIDFIELDER

LOWDOWN! Rochemback was solid in his first season after joining from Sporting Lisbon. The Brazil man picked up three assists and hit two goals. His first league strike was special – in a 3-0 win over Chelsea!

PLAYED	22	STARS	1	AVE. RATING	6.41

MARK SCHWARZER ⭐5
⚽ AGE: 33 ⚽ POSITION: GOALKEEPER

LOWDOWN! Schwarzer did enough to hold on to his No.1 shirt at Boro. He was under pressure from Brad Jones, but some quality displays kept him in. His big-match experience was vital as Boro hit mid-table safety!

PLAYED	27	STARS	0	AVE. RATING	6.37

NEWCASTLE!

SCOTT PARKER ⭐1
⚽ AGE: 25 ⚽ POSITION: MIDFIELDER

LOWDOWN! Newcastle wished Parker's season hadn't finished in March through injury – he was superb! With nine Star Ratings in 26 matches, Parker always gave 100 per cent and became the new fans' favourite!

PLAYED	26	STARS	9	AVE. RATING	6.81

SHAY GIVEN ⭐2
⚽ AGE: 30 ⚽ POSITION: GOALKEEPER

LOWDOWN! Given is one of the best 'keepers in the Prem, and was in top form again. The Republic Of Ireland star didn't miss a game for Newcastle and made some vital saves, including a penalty against Aston Villa!

PLAYED	38	STARS	2	AVE. RATING	6.51

EMRE ⭐3
⚽ AGE: 26 ⚽ POSITION: MIDFIELDER

LOWDOWN! Another Newcastle new boy who suffered through injury. Emre did well enough in just 20 games to be one of the team's top men. The Turkey midfielder scored two goals – one against big rivals Sunderland!

PLAYED	20	STARS	2	AVE. RATING	6.40

STEPHEN CARR ⭐4
⚽ AGE: 30 ⚽ POSITION: DEFENDER

LOWDOWN! Carr missed two months of action between January and March, but his right-back displays stood out a mile. Clearly Newcastle's most consistent defender, his red card against Chelsea was disappointing.

PLAYED	19	STARS	0	AVE. RATING	6.32

NOLBERTO SOLANO ⭐5
⚽ AGE: 31 ⚽ POSITION: MIDFIELDER

LOWDOWN! Solano returned from Aston Villa in August and, although his debut wasn't until October, the Peru star showed his class. He hit six goals in the Premiership, including the winner at home against Arsenal!

PLAYED	29	STARS	1	AVE. RATING	6.15

PORTSMOUTH!

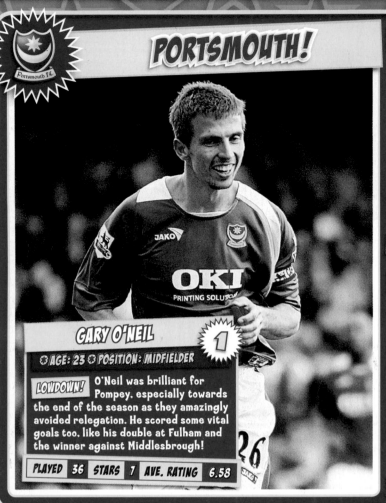

GARY O'NEIL
⚙ AGE: 23 ⚙ POSITION: MIDFIELDER

LOWDOWN! O'Neil was brilliant for Pompey, especially towards the end of the season as they amazingly avoided relegation. He scored some vital goals too, like his double at Fulham and the winner against Middlesbrough!

| PLAYED | 36 | STARS | 7 | AVE. RATING | 6.58 |

DEJAN STEFANOVIC — 2
⚙ AGE: 31 ⚙ POSITION: DEFENDER

LOWDOWN! Stefanovic has bags of experience, and used it to good effect when Pompey were battling relegation! The tough centre-back was in commanding form as he led the team away from the bottom three.

| PLAYED | 28 | STARS | 2 | AVE. RATING | 6.54 |

LOMANA LUA LUA — 3
⚙ AGE: 25 ⚙ POSITION: STRIKER

LOWDOWN! Tricky striker Lomana Lua Lua was a major reason Pompey stayed up! His goals dried up in the middle of the season, but he finished strongly with four in his last four games before injury struck.

| PLAYED | 25 | STARS | 2 | AVE. RATING | 6.48 |

LINVOY PRIMUS — 4
⚙ AGE: 33 ⚙ POSITION: DEFENDER

LOWDOWN! Primus rarely played before December, but after that, he was rarely out of the team! His return to the side led to an upturn in Pompey's form, and he loved having Harry Redknapp back in charge!

| PLAYED | 20 | STARS | 0 | AVE. RATING | 6.45 |

PEDRO MENDES — 5
⚙ AGE: 27 ⚙ POSITION: MIDFIELDER

LOWDOWN! Mendes was snapped up from Spurs in January and made a major impact. The Portugal midfielder scored two crackers against Man. City in a 2-1 win that sparked a brilliant seven-game unbeaten run!

| PLAYED | 20 | STARS | 2 | AVE. RATING | 6.40 |

SUNDERLAND!

JULIO ARCA
✱ AGE: 25 ✱ POSITION: DEFENDER

LOWDOWN! Arca was Sunderland's left-back last season, but with 54 crosses, two assists and a goal in the win over Boro, the Argentinian was ace going forward too! He was booked five times during the campaign.

| PLAYED | 24 | STARS | 1 | AVE. RATING | 6.50 |

DEAN WHITEHEAD — 2
✱ AGE: 24 ✱ POSITION: MIDFIELDER

LOWDOWN! Whitehead was a bargain signing for Sunderland in 2004, costing £150,000 from Oxford! He was in good form for The Black Cats last season, playing 37 games, scoring three goals and providing six assists!

| PLAYED | 37 | STARS | 3 | AVE. RATING | 6.39 |

GARY BREEN — 3
✱ AGE: 32 ✱ POSITION: DEFENDER

LOWDOWN! Big centre-back Breen made 75 clearances and 26 blocks for Sunderland, but couldn't prevent relegation. He scored in the 1-1 draw with West Brom, but was sent off in the 2-1 defeat at Man. City.

| PLAYED | 35 | STARS | 1 | AVE. RATING | 6.17 |

NYRON NOSWORTHY — 4
✱ AGE: 25 ✱ POSITION: DEFENDER

LOWDOWN! A freebie from Gillingham, Nosworthy was thrown straight into Premiership action last season! The powerful right-back held his own against tough teams and was one of Sunderland's best players.

| PLAYED | 30 | STARS | 0 | AVE. RATING | 6.15 |

DANNY COLLINS — 5
✱ AGE: 26 ✱ POSITION: DEFENDER

LOWDOWN! Another bargain buy from non-league footy. Collins had a season to remember! He won his first international cap for Wales and scored his first Premiership goal on the last day of the season!

| PLAYED | 23 | STARS | 0 | AVE. RATING | 6.12 |

TOTTENHAM!

MICHAEL CARRICK
⊙ AGE: 25 ⊙ POSITION: MIDFIELDER

LOWDOWN! An average of 6.89, added to eight Star Ratings, says everything about Carrick's fine season. The England midfielder played some excellent stuff for Tottenham, with two goals, six assists and 91 crosses!

| PLAYED | 35 | STARS | 8 | AVE. RATING | 6.89 |

MICHAEL DAWSON [2]
⊙ AGE: 22 ⊙ POSITION: DEFENDER

LOWDOWN! The ex-Nottingham Forest centre-back was only just nudged out of top spot and enjoyed a great season. He made 62 clearances, 31 blocks, picked up two assists – and played for the England B team too!

| PLAYED | 32 | STARS | 3 | AVE. RATING | 6.88 |

LEDLEY KING [3]
⊙ AGE: 25 ⊙ POSITION: DEFENDER

LOWDOWN! King formed a solid duo with Dawson, until a foot injury ended his season in April and ruined his chances of playing for England at the World Cup. Ledley scored three goals in the league, too!

| PLAYED | 26 | STARS | 3 | AVE. RATING | 6.88 |

PAUL ROBINSON [4]
⊙ AGE: 26 ⊙ POSITION: GOALKEEPER

LOWDOWN! Robinson was a busy boy last season, playing in 38 games and guiding Spurs to the UEFA Cup before heading off to the World Cup with England. With 13 clean sheets, Robbo kept things tight at the back!

| PLAYED | 38 | STARS | 1 | AVE. RATING | 6.63 |

EDGAR DAVIDS [5]
⊙ AGE: 33 ⊙ POSITION: MIDFIELDER

LOWDOWN! There was a buzz at White Hart Lane when Davids joined Spurs, and the Dutchman didn't disappoint. Although he only scored one goal – in a 2-1 win at Wigan – he was in typical all-action mode!

| PLAYED | 31 | STARS | 5 | AVE. RATING | 6.52 |

WEST BROM!

TOMASZ KUSZCZAK
⊙ AGE: 24 ⊙ POSITION: GOALKEEPER

LOWDOWN! Tomasz grabbed the gloves when on loan 'keeper Chris Kirkland was struck down with injury, and he played a blinder! The Poland star was kept busy as Albion went down, but he did pick up two Star Ratings.

| PLAYED | 28 | STARS | 2 | AVE. RATING | 6.50 |

CURTIS DAVIES [2]
⊙ AGE: 21 ⊙ POSITION: DEFENDER

LOWDOWN! Davies was signed from Luton for £3 million and soon got used to life in the Premiership. The centre-back turned in some cool displays in defence and scored twice, against Charlton and Tottenham!

| PLAYED | 33 | STARS | 0 | AVE. RATING | 6.43 |

MARTIN ALBRECHTSEN [3]
⊙ AGE: 27 ⊙ POSITION: DEFENDER

LOWDOWN! The Denmark defender was a versatile star in West Brom's defence, doing a solid job at right-back or centre-back. He made 29 clearances and five blocks, and his goal bagged all three points at Wigan!

| PLAYED | 31 | STARS | 0 | AVE. RATING | 6.33 |

PAUL ROBINSON [4]
⊙ AGE: 27 ⊙ POSITION: DEFENDER

LOWDOWN! Robinson was a West Brom favourite last season, with his tough tackles and charging runs! With 48 crosses and three assists, he was an attacking threat, but he also picked up seven yellow cards!

| PLAYED | 33 | STARS | 1 | AVE. RATING | 6.29 |

NEIL CLEMENT [5]
⊙ AGE: 27 ⊙ POSITION: DEFENDER

LOWDOWN! Clement has been one of West Brom's best players for years, so it was no surprise to see him in the top five. Blessed with a great left foot, he delivered ten crosses and scored in the 4-0 stuffing of Everton!

| PLAYED | 31 | STARS | 5 | AVE. RATING | 6.27 |

WEST HAM!

DANIEL GABBIDON
* AGE: 27 * POSITION: DEFENDER

LOWDOWN! Signed from Cardiff City, Gabbidon was outstanding in his first season in the top flight. The Wales defender was a powerful figure at the heart of The Hammers' back four and not many strikers got past him!

| PLAYED | 32 | STARS | 2 | AVE. RATING | 6.84 |

ANTON FERDINAND — 2
* AGE: 21 * POSITION: DEFENDER

LOWDOWN! Rio's younger brother was a Premiership star in his own right last season, thanks to a string of impressive games. Anton played well whether at right-back or centre-back, and scored a couple of goals too!

| PLAYED | 33 | STARS | 0 | AVE. RATING | 6.70 |

PAUL KONCHESKY — 3
* AGE: 25 * POSITION: DEFENDER

LOWDOWN! A £1.5 million signing from Charlton, Konchesky's season started badly with a red card against Newcastle, but he soon settled down and missed just one game. The left-back made a whopping 111 crosses!

| PLAYED | 37 | STARS | 2 | AVE. RATING | 6.59 |

YOSSI BENAYOUN — 4
* AGE: 26 * POSITION: MIDFIELDER

LOWDOWN! Benayoun added flair and class to West Ham's right wing, scoring five goals and supplying seven assists for The Hammers. The Israeli's tricky feet and quick turns were a nightmare for defenders!

| PLAYED | 34 | STARS | 1 | AVE. RATING | 6.56 |

NIGEL REO-COKER — 5
* AGE: 22 * POSITION: MIDFIELDER

LOWDOWN! West Ham's young captain was in brilliant form last season! He scored in the opening game against Blackburn and his energy, passing and leadership were vital. He chipped in with five Prem goals, too!

| PLAYED | 31 | STARS | 2 | AVE. RATING | 6.52 |

WIGAN!

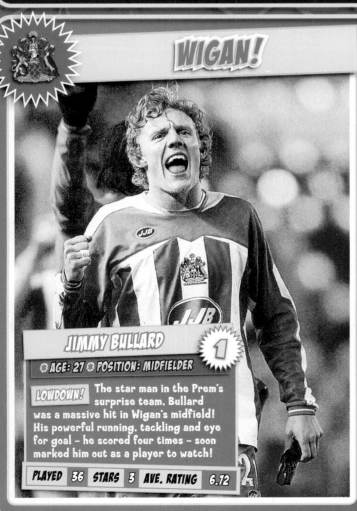

JIMMY BULLARD
* AGE: 27 * POSITION: MIDFIELDER

LOWDOWN! The star man in the Prem's surprise team, Bullard was a massive hit in Wigan's midfield! His powerful running, tackling and eye for goal – he scored four times – soon marked him out as a player to watch!

| PLAYED | 36 | STARS | 3 | AVE. RATING | 6.72 |

HENRI CAMARA — 2
* AGE: 29 * POSITION: STRIKER

LOWDOWN! Camara had tasted relegation at Wolves and Southampton, but his 12 Premiership goals helped Wigan to safety with ease. He scored a superb hat-trick in a 3-0 win over Charlton in December!

| PLAYED | 29 | STARS | 3 | AVE. RATING | 6.66 |

PASCAL CHIMBONDA — 3
* AGE: 27 * POSITION: DEFENDER

LOWDOWN! Chimbonda arrived from Bastia as an unknown, but he was excellent at right-back and quickly caught the eye! His all-action displays earned him a spot in France's World Cup squad as well!

| PLAYED | 37 | STARS | 1 | AVE. RATING | 6.59 |

MIKE POLLITT — 4
* AGE: 34 * POSITION: GOALKEEPER

LOWDOWN! Pollitt has played for loads of lower league clubs, and was a £200,000 bargain signing from Rotherham. He faced competition from John Filan for the No.1 spot, but he did enough to impress boss Paul Jewell!

| PLAYED | 24 | STARS | 1 | AVE. RATING | 6.58 |

GRAHAM KAVANAGH — 5
* AGE: 32 * POSITION: MIDFIELDER

LOWDOWN! Kav gave Wigan's midfield much-needed experience last season, especially after Damien Francis was injured. He delivered 38 crosses, but most of his best work was when he protected the back four.

| PLAYED | 35 | STARS | 5 | AVE. RATING | 6.54 |

WORLD SUPERSTARS!

GIANLUCA ZAMBROTTA
ITALY

INJURY!
A clash in training has left you with a sore ankle! Miss two turns!

ESTADIO MESTALLA, VALENCIA
Use both dice and roll a 9 to score!

MARACANA, RIO DE JANEIRO
Use one dice and roll a 3 to score!

ANFIELD, LIVERPOOL
Use one dice and roll a 5 to score!

GOODISON PARK, LIVERPOOL
Use both dice and roll a 7 to score!

RIVERSIDE STADIUM, MIDDLESBROUGH
Use both dice and roll a 2 to score!

OUR ACE NEW GAME...
GOAL MAC

YELLOW CARD!
Doh! You've upset the ref and picked up a booking! Miss a turn!

THE NEW WEMBLEY
You've made it! Use both dice to roll a 12 to score!
Once you've scored three goals, you've won!

STADE DE FRANCE, PARIS
Use one dice and roll a 1 to score!

CITY OF MANCHESTER STADIUM, MANCHESTER
Use both dice and roll a 6 to score!

VILLA PARK, BIRMINGHAM
Use one dice and roll a 4 to score!

START HERE!

ROLL BOTH DICE AND SEE WHERE YOU LAND!

NOU CAMP, BARCELONA
Use both dice and roll a 12 to score!

OLD TRAFFORD, MANCHESTER
Use both dice and roll a 9 to score!

STAMFORD BRIDGE, CHELSEA
Use one dice and roll a 4 to score!

SAN SIRO, MILAN
Use both dice and roll a 4 to score!

TRANSFER!
Chelsea splash the cash to buy you! Move to Stamford Bridge!

ST. JAMES' PARK, NEWCASTLE
Use one dice and roll a 6 to score!

LOST BOOTS!
You've lost your lucky scoring boots! Use one dice and roll a 6 to carry on!

WESTFALEN STADION, DORTMUND
Use both dice and roll an 8 to score!

RED CARD!
Disaster – you've been sent off! Use both dice and roll a 3 to carry on!

...HINE!

Have you got what it takes to be a superstar striker and score goals in the world's greatest stadiums? Get your mates together, grab a pencil, pick up those dice and prove it!

HOW TO PLAY!

⭐ Roll the dice to move around the board and carefully follow the instructions on the squares!

⭐ Mark off which stadiums you score in by ticking them off on the scoreboard!

⭐ Once you've bagged a goal in each stadium, move to the new Wembley! You may have to move around the board a few times to score in every ground!

⭐ The first player to score a hat-trick at Wembley is the winner! Good luck!

STADIO DELLE ALPI, TURIN
Use both dice and roll a 6 to score!

YOU'RE ON FIRE!
You can't stop scoring goals! Take an extra turn!

THE SCOREBOARD! THE SCOREBOARD! THE SCOREBOARD!

PLAYER ONE!

	VILLA PARK, BIRMINGHAM	CITY OF MANCHESTER STADIUM	STADE DE FRANCE, PARIS	RIVERSIDE STADIUM, BORO
MARACANA, RIO DE JANEIRO	ANFIELD, LIVERPOOL	GOODISON PARK, LIVERPOOL	ESTADIO MESTALLA, VALENCIA	ST. JAMES' PARK, NEWCASTLE	WESTFALEN STADION, DORTMUND
STADIO DELLE ALPI, TURIN	WHITE HART LANE, TOTTENHAM	EMIRATES STADIUM, ARSENAL	ALLIANZ ARENA, MUNICH	OLYMPIC STADIUM, BERLIN	BERNABEU, MADRID
SAN SIRO, MILAN	STAMFORD BRIDGE, CHELSEA	OLD TRAFFORD, MANCHESTER	NOU CAMP, BARCELONA	THE NEW WEMBLEY! ✓ ✓ ✓

PLAYER TWO!

	VILLA PARK, BIRMINGHAM	CITY OF MANCHESTER STADIUM	STADE DE FRANCE, PARIS	RIVERSIDE STADIUM, BORO
MARACANA, RIO DE JANEIRO	ANFIELD, LIVERPOOL	GOODISON PARK, LIVERPOOL	ESTADIO MESTALLA, VALENCIA	ST JAMES' PARK, NEWCASTLE	WESTFALEN STADION, DORTMUND
STADIO DELLE ALPI, TURIN	WHITE HART LANE, TOTTENHAM	EMIRATES STADIUM, ARSENAL	ALLIANZ ARENA, MUNICH	OLYMPIC STADIUM, BERLIN	BERNABEU, MADRID
SAN SIRO, MILAN	STAMFORD BRIDGE, CHELSEA	OLD TRAFFORD, MANCHESTER	NOU CAMP, BARCELONA	THE NEW WEMBLEY! ✓ ✓ ✓

PLAYER THREE!

	VILLA PARK, BIRMINGHAM	CITY OF MANCHESTER STADIUM	STADE DE FRANCE, PARIS	RIVERSIDE STADIUM, BORO
MARACANA, RIO DE JANEIRO	ANFIELD, LIVERPOOL	GOODISON PARK, LIVERPOOL	ESTADIO MESTALLA, VALENCIA	ST JAMES' PARK, NEWCASTLE	WESTFALEN STADION, DORTMUND
STADIO DELLE ALPI, TURIN	WHITE HART LANE, TOTTENHAM	EMIRATES STADIUM, ARSENAL	ALLIANZ ARENA, MUNICH	OLYMPIC STADIUM, BERLIN	BERNABEU, MADRID
SAN SIRO, MILAN	STAMFORD BRIDGE, CHELSEA	OLD TRAFFORD, MANCHESTER	NOU CAMP, BARCELONA	THE NEW WEMBLEY! ✓ ✓ ✓

PLAYER FOUR!

	VILLA PARK, BIRMINGHAM	CITY OF MANCHESTER STADIUM	STADE DE FRANCE, PARIS	RIVERSIDE STADIUM, BORO
MARACANA, RIO DE JANEIRO	ANFIELD, LIVERPOOL	GOODISON PARK, LIVERPOOL	ESTADIO MESTALLA, VALENCIA	ST JAMES' PARK, NEWCASTLE	WESTFALEN STADION, DORTMUND
STADIO DELLE ALPI, TURIN	WHITE HART LANE, TOTTENHAM	EMIRATES STADIUM, ARSENAL	ALLIANZ ARENA, MUNICH	OLYMPIC STADIUM, BERLIN	BERNABEU, MADRID
SAN SIRO, MILAN	STAMFORD BRIDGE, CHELSEA	OLD TRAFFORD, MANCHESTER	NOU CAMP, BARCELONA	THE NEW WEMBLEY! ✓ ✓ ✓

SUSPENDED!
You've picked up too many bookings during the season! Miss a turn!

WHITE HART LANE, TOTTENHAM
Use both dice and roll a 7 to score!

EMIRATES STADIUM, ARSENAL
Use one dice and roll a 6 to score!

PENALTY MISS!
You miss a penalty and lose all your confidence! Go back to Villa Park!

BERNABEU, MADRID
Use both dice and roll an 11 to score!

OLYMPIC STADIUM, BERLIN
Use both dice and roll a 10 to score!

CALL-UP!
Steve McClaren has called you up to the England team! Take two extra turns!

ALLIANZ ARENA, MUNICH
Use one dice and roll a 5 to score!

MATCHMAN'S QUIZ

PHEW! THAT WAS SOME TOUGH QUIZZIN'! HOW DID YOU DO? LOOK THROUGH THE ANSWERS AN' ADD UP YER TOTAL TO SEE IF YER A FOOTY BRAINBUSTER!

0-50!
FOOTY FLOP!
That's rubbish! You need to read MATCH every week!

51-100!
BENCH WARMER!
Come on! This is pants! Step up your game!

101-150!
PROMISING YOUNGSTER!
Unlucky! A bit of hard work and you could make it!

151-200!
INTERNATIONAL CALL-UP!
Good effort! You're almost ready for the big time!

201-250!
CHAMPIONS LEAGUE KING!
Top footy knowledge! Yer one of the best around!

251-300!
WORLD CUP WINNER!
Awesome! You're the top player! Wicked stuff!

PREMIERSHIP!
PAGE 42!   MY SCORE   /60

THE KNOWLEDGE!
1. Alan Shearer
2. Athletic – Charlton & Wigan
3. Aston Villa
4. In the top four
5. Blackburn

PERCY'S PLAYERS!
Robin van Persie

MEDAL MOUNTAIN!
Arjen Robben

SPOT THE SPIES!
Rafa Benitez, Martin Jol, David Moyes, Stuart Pearce & Gareth Southgate

FOOTY FRIENDS!
West Ham

TURNSTILE TOTALS!
1. C
2. B
3. D
4. A
5. E

ANSWERS!

LA LIGA!
PAGE 54! MY SCORE [ ] /60

NATIONAL DRESS!
Carlos Puyol

BADGE IT!
Villarreal

BEHIND THE BULL!
David Beckham

KINGS OF SPAIN!
1. C
2. D
3. B
4. A
5. E

GIANLUCA ZAMBROTTA QUIZ!
1. Italy
2. 29
3. Juventus
4. Lilian Thuram
5. One

CROSSWORD!
NOUCAMP
ARGENTINA
MADRID
SAMUEL
BARCELONA
DAVID
VIGO
GALACTICOS
DE VILLA
VALENCIA
CASILLAS

GOALDEN WORD
Ronaldo

SERIE A!
PAGE 66! MY SCORE [ ] /60

BADGE IT!
Parma

SERIE SALES!
1. Fabio Cannavaro - Real Madrid
2. Andriy Shevchenko - Chelsea
3. Marco Bresciano - Palermo
4. Gianluca Zambrotta - Barcelona
5. Fabio Grosso - Inter Milan

TRANSFER TRACKER!
1998-1999 - Lazio
1999-2005 - Inter Milan

DREAM TEAM!
GK: Angelo Peruzzi
RB: Cafu
CB: Philippe Mexes
CB: Marco Materazzi
LB: Matteo Ferrari
RM: Stefano Fiore
CM: Esteban Cambiasso
CM: Francesco Totti
ST: Alberto Gilardino
ST: Simone Inzaghi

SPOT THE DIFFERENCE!
1. Badges missing from Milan player;
2. No text on billboard; 3. Ref's shirt is
green; 4. Diadora boot logos are red;
5. Arm missing on the right

STAR NAMES!
Inter, Roma or Siena

WORLD FOOTY!
PAGE 70! MY SCORE [ ] /60

CRUNCH TIME!
1. B
2. C
3. E
4. A
5. D

ARGEN-TEAM-A!
Independiente
Boca Juniors
River Plate
Newell's Old Boys
Estudiantes

FREDDY ADU QUIZ!
1. 17
2. DC United
3. False
4. Ghana
5. Nike

DR FOOTY'S FACTS AND FIB!
Line 1 is false

HEAD OF TWO HALVES!
Fabien Barthez & Juninho

WORDFIT!

```
        M A   Y O                 W
        A     O R       W A N
        L                     N
  P O B O R S K Y     A N       B E A S L E Y
        U             C         C
        D             H A       W
  R I V A L D O       O   B       H
        E             B     V E R O N
          L I N D E R O T H       I
            G               M     N
  D O N O V A N     U D           A   S
          U     D                 N   T
          M               E D M A N   E
                      G       I   N   V
  F R E I           A L       E   I   E Z
        J             L               G
          F R E D   V A N D E R V A A R T
        L             S
              K J N E
              K Ø L L E R
```

FOOTBALL LEAGUE!
PAGE 76! MY SCORE [ ] /60

GROUNDED!
Leicester

PERCY'S PLAYERS!
DJ Campbell

SPOT THE BALL
F4

ENGLAND YOUNG GUNS!
1. C
2. B
3. D
4. A
5. E

LEAGUE OF NATIONS!
1. Earnshaw - D
2. Forssell - C
3. Rasiak - E
4. Healy - A
5. Hoefkens - B

FOOTBALL LEAGUE MATCH-UP!
A-2-W
B-4-V
C-3-Z
D-5-X
E-1-Y

WORLD SUPERSTARS!

MATCH!

MIROSLAV KLOSE
GERMANY